Tammy Sandthus
— 1969 —

FORBES CARLILE ON SWIMMING

Forbes Carlile
on Swimming

PELHAM BOOKS

First published by
PELHAM BOOKS LTD
26 Bloomsbury Street
*London, W.C.*1
OCTOBER 1963
SECOND IMPRESSION APRIL 1964
THIRD IMPRESSION AUGUST 1965
FOURTH IMPRESSION OCTOBER 1966
FIFTH IMPRESSION APRIL 1968

Reproduced and printed lithographically in Great
Britain by the Hollen Street Press Ltd., Slough and
bound by James Burn at Esher, Surrey.

Contents

Illustrations

Preface

For more than 20 years Forbes Carlile has been one of Australia's leading coaches, first as an amateur when he was a lecturer in Human Physiology at the University of Sydney, and since 1955 as a full-time professional coach. He has played an important part in raising Australian swimmers to their present-day standard.

Although in Australia Mr Carlile has been recognised as a leader in scientific training, it was not until 1962 that the interest of the swimming world abroad suddenly focussed on him following the outstanding success of the Dutch swimmers at the European championships in Leipzig. Appointed as National Coach for Holland, with his wife Ursula (also a swimming coach) he lived in the Netherlands for six months, training the Dutch team. During this time they reshaped Dutch attitudes to competitive swimming. Traditional ideas were modified or thrown out, and new methods (Carlile's) were introduced.

The amazing success of the Dutch swimmers at Leipzig is history now. From 23 competing nations Holland had its greatest international scoop, winning 16 medals. The men swimmers rose from 'nowhere' to be in world class and the girls swept all before them to gain European swimming supremacy.

The most significant advance which puzzled the expert observers was that every member of the Dutch team recorded his or her best personal performance, at the most critical time, that being in the finals of their big events at Leipzig.

What is Forbes Carlile's magic?

Here you can read how he does it. Swimmers and coaches will find many of their questions answered in this book – it is indeed a most important contribution to the literature of swimming.

S. B. GRANGE
Vice-Chairman of the
F.I.N.A. Technical Committee

SYDNEY
AUSTRALIA

Introduction

I have divided this book into three parts. *Part I* is essentially practical. If a swimmer bases his preparation on these instructions I believe he will be happy with the results. In our talks with many coaches throughout the world we have found their greatest single problem is knowing how to prepare swimmers for making peak performances at the right time. We shall therefore consider this matter fully, believing it to be at the very core of successful training for competitive swimmers

Part II is of a more scientific nature to satisfy the serious student of swimming who asks the whys and wherefors of training methods. This section gives the scientific background for many of the instructions in *Part I*. Here we consider in detail our research on physiological changes occurring in the swimmer during training and over-training.

Part III deals with another important practical question, that of coaching swimming techniques. I have tackled this by way of an historical approach because much of our knowledge about swimming styles is based fundamentally on the experiments and methods of competitive swimmers of the past. I have found that people are always interested to hear about the early swimmers, about the great John Weissmuller, or the Japanese swimmers who swept all before them in the 1930s. More than 15 years ago I started collecting the historical data which stems from varied sources. Many of the Australian 'old timers' with whom I talked and corresponded have since died, but they, and many others of whom you will read, have contributed substantially to competitive swimming as we know it today.

I have tried to make this an *original* book, not merely a rehash of all that has been written before. I have tried not to 'dazzle' you with too much science but to concentrate on the most significant factors and on recent trends in competitive swimming, which *I* believe make up good training and good technique.

Above all this book is written to serve as an up-to-date, *practical guide* for competitive swimmers and their coaches.

PART I
TRAINING AND REACHING
A PEAK

CHAPTER ONE

Training — A Year-Round Project

LET us get this straight from the start – preparation for top
competitive swimming must be a well planned, year-round
process. The days have long passed when you could hope to
prepare for a month or two each year, and remain a top swimmer. The fact is that today practically all Olympic finalists swim
for nine or ten months of the year, and most do out-of-the-water
strengthening exercises as well.

Training should be as scientific and organised as we can make
it. Above all we must keep a clear idea of our goal, *what* particular events we are training for, and *when* we want to reach our
peak performances. If you think that the swimmer should be
able to turn on just about his best times *all the year round*, then I
believe you are mistaken and that trying to do this will result in
the swimmer *never* being able to give his best possible performance. In planning training, the swimmer must aim for *one*, or at
the most *two* peaks each year. The main reason for this is that
top performance requires two or three months of *very* strenuous
training. In this time of heavy stress, before a 'tapering-off' of
the training (about which we shall speak later) the body is not
ready to make a maximum effort. During this period of very
strenuous training coaches usually find that times become worse.
We can't have it both ways. We can't expect the swimmer to give
peak performances and at the same time carry out the tremendous day-by-day training load which we now know to be
necessary for outstanding results in the long run.

In recent years swimmers have broken world records with
both 'one-peak' and 'two-peak' training schedules. Australians
Dawn Fraser, John and Ilsa Konrads, David Theile, Kevin
Berry and others have done it on a 'one-peak' schedule, but
world records have also fallen to Chet Jastremski, Tom Stock
and other Americans who regularly reached two peaks in the

15

year, one in April for the U.S.A. Collegiate or National Indoor Championships and another in August for the National Outdoor Titles.

Because of competitions held nearly every alternate year in the Northern Hemisphere summer (Commonwealth and Olympic Games), the Australian system for a while now has required a periodic change to a 'two-peak' training plan, and I believe that this force of circumstances has led Australians to an almost ideal schedule with half a season away from strenuous competition every second year. It is my opinion that most *young* swimmers are better off training for a one-peak year, rather than being expected to prepare for periods of serious competition twice or more during the year.

I believe that for world record breaking the *basic* training plan should be one aimed at preparation for a *one-peak* year, and discussions in this book will, in the main, be centred around this approach. In Figure 1 you will see that the first three columns refer to such a one-peak year. The fourth column shows the relative amounts of swimming suggested within a *two*-peak year (which is a modified one-peak programme).

PLAN FOR A ONE-PEAK YEAR

Period 1. *Games, Exercises and Swimming*

In the Southern Hemisphere (Australia, New Zealand, South Africa, etc.) this will start in April. North of the Equator (in Europe and the U.S.A.) this first period will usually start in November. Remember we are discussing a one-peak year with big races in the summer. Period 1 is the time when there should be a rest from hard swimming, or as I look at it, a time when the specific parts of the nervous system which are involved in swimming should be given a chance to recover from strenuous training and racing. However, the fitness of cardio-vascular system and the muscular strength should be kept at as high a level as possible with games, running, weight-training and flexibility exercises. In order to retain some 'swimming condition' a little should be done in this period, perhaps two or three easy swims each week.

In my opinion the cross-country running, which for years played an important part in the training of Dutch girl swimmers under Coach Jan Stender in Hilversum (Holland), contributed

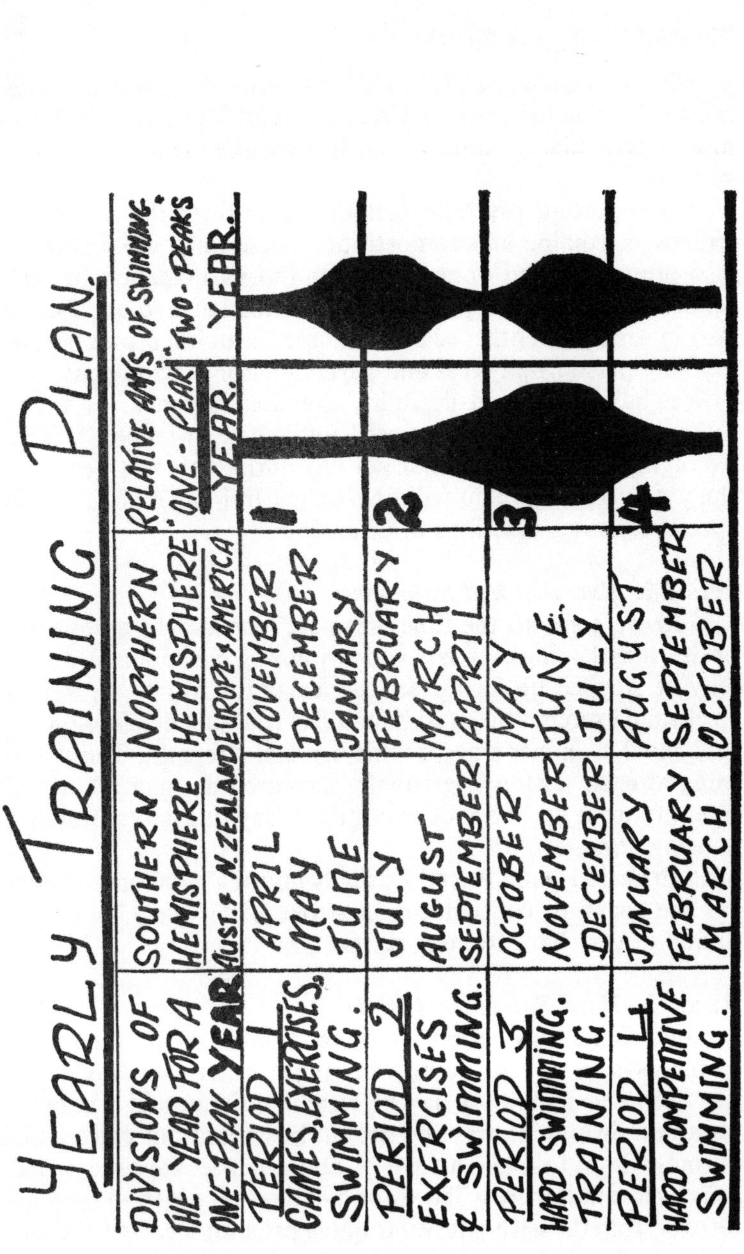

YEARLY TRAINING PLAN.

DIVISIONS OF THE YEAR FOR A ONE-PEAK YEAR	SOUTHERN HEMISPHERE (Aust. & N. Zealand)	NORTHERN HEMISPHERE (Europe & America)	RELATIVE AMTS OF SWIMMING 'ONE-PEAK' YEAR / 'TWO-PEAKS' YEAR
PERIOD 1 GAMES, EXERCISES, SWIMMING.	APRIL MAY JUNE	NOVEMBER DECEMBER JANUARY	1
PERIOD 2 EXERCISES & SWIMMING.	JULY AUGUST SEPTEMBER	FEBRUARY MARCH APRIL	2
PERIOD 3 HARD SWIMMING TRAINING.	OCTOBER NOVEMBER DECEMBER	MAY JUNE JULY	3
PERIOD 4 HARD COMPETITIVE SWIMMING.	JANUARY FEBRUARY MARCH	AUGUST SEPTEMBER OCTOBER	4

Fig. 1

greatly to their success in the early 1950s when six world record holders lived in the one street in Hilversum! These girls certainly maintained highly trained cardio-vascular and respiratory systems.

It is important psychologically to relax from the tension of strenuous training and competition. These three months or so also present a good opportunity for full participation in such school games as hockey, football, basketball and so on. Taking part in games and other school activities is an important part of a young person's physical and psychological development.

Weight training and flexibility exercises designed for swimmers may be gradually increased until some swimmers will be averaging about half an hour per day during this first period of the year's training. You will find weight training schedules and special exercises described in Chapter 5.

Period 2. *Exercises and Swimming*

Now we come to the time when we increase the amount of both strengthening exercises and swimming. Swimming training may be stepped up to one session a day for five or six days a week, and exercises up to an hour a day (but this depends on the individual swimmer's needs – his age and strength). The swimming at each session is gradually increased in quantity and in intensity until up to about two miles a day of interval training is being done.

Both Period 1 and Period 2 usually afford a good opportunity for the coach to concentrate on stroke techniques, before the period of very hard training starts.

Period 3. *Hard Swimming Training*

Now comes the period of three months or so when the emphasis is on very strenuous work in the water with only about ten to fifteen minutes a day of weight training and flexibility exercises. Swimming training should be carried out twice daily on most days, to make a total of about ten sessions per week. This means that there will be four half days on which to rest and recover from the hard interval training programme. One of these half days should be used each week for time trials or club races. Almost from the start of the hard training period I believe that club races or inter-club competitions should be held regularly.

At Ryde, our Australian headquarters in Sydney, these races are conducted by amateur officials (mostly parents of swimmers) for boys and girls on Saturday mornings and create great interest and enthusiasm amongst the 600 or so club members, the majority of whom we coach. As soon as they are able to swim 25 yards, the children can enter a wide variety of races at all styles and distances. These regular club meetings, besides being good fun, are the ideal way for swimmers to gain experience in racing. A coach can learn much about his pupils by watching them race, and both coach and pupils will benefit greatly by these 'dress-rehearsals' for the more important championships later in the season. Being relatively unimportant, these weekly club races and local inter-club competitions are seldom permitted to interfere with the ordinary routine of hard training, in fact it is not unusual for swimmers to enter a club race immediately after a training session of two miles or so.

During this period, where possible, swimming should be done outdoors in the 50 metre or 55 yard course. I know, of course, that in many places it is quite impossible to swim outdoors regularly for a full three months, and then I believe that it is much better to swim indoors in 25 metre or even 20 yard courses rather than put up with very cold conditions. It has been my experience that a few weeks of long-course training before a big competition is enough to accustom experienced swimmers to these racing conditions. I am inclined to think that far too much has been made of the need to train in the 50 m course. I think it is better to settle for reasonably comfortable warm water indoors than uncomfortable freezing conditions outside. Most *swimmers* will back me up in this, especially, my squad at Ryde when early in the season I have to drive them back, blue and shivering, to finish their training! Far better five miles of training *indoors* than an 'heroic' one mile outdoors.

In Australia, because we have very few indoor pools, practically *all* our training is done outdoors, but in Holland and in Europe generally, from what I have seen, swimmers are forced to train indoors much of the time.

Period 4. *Hard Competitive Swimming*
Here we enter the period of important races and 'tapering-off' (the subject of Chapters 3 and 4). From time to time, between

important races, the quantity and intensity of swimming training will be increased for a week or so and then eased off again before the next important race.

If you look at the fourth column in our diagrammatic representation of the Yearly Training Plan, you will see that in a two-peak year all the four periods are necessarily shortened and that nowhere is as much swimming carried out as during the hard training phase of the one-peak year. However, in both plans over the complete year there is a *large amount* of swimming, for the older top swimmer nowadays, up to 500 or 600 miles or more in the twelve months.

The keynote of successful training to my mind is the idea of *working to a peak*. There is much more to good training than covering as many miles as possible.

In the next chapter we shall take up the important consideration of how we might construct a training programme.

CHAPTER TWO

How to Train

I AM never happy about setting out a training programme, mainly because we can *never* stick to the details of one ourselves. There are so many factors which may change, the water may become very cold in outdoor pools, many of the group may be 'worn-out,' examination time may mean that swimming must be cut – there are all kinds of situations which could call for a change in the programme.

The programmes which I shall suggest here are examples of the *type* of training we use at Ryde (Sydney) in an outdoor 55-yard pool, but in detail our programme is seldom the same for two consecutive days.

If you have swimmers of various ages and abilities you will probably find, as we do, that it is best to divide them into four groups for training.

These groups we might call Top Older Swimmers, Top Younger Swimmers (10 to 12 years) and Intermediate (10 years to 18 or so). A fourth group we call the 'Improver' squad and it is comprised of young swimmers who have just learned to swim. They are still learning the basic techniques of all strokes, as well as learning starts and turns and aiming at being able to enter club races as soon as possible. We find this incentive important.

Because this is a book on advanced swimming we shall only consider here programmes for Top Older, Top Younger, and Intermediate swimmers. Many Intermediate swimmers, will, during the season, move up into one of the higher groups.

During the hard training period we run ten or eleven sessions of training each week, twice daily, but with 'rest' afternoons on Fridays. Sometimes a *full* rest day is taken off each week, depending on the apparent needs of the individual swimmers. We have no set rules about this.

Before setting out schedules of training there are some things

I want to explain. The bare programmes would be of little use to you without these explanations.

We have found that most swimmers, particularly those on the hardest programme, need to be continually encouraged and at times 'bullied' into coming regularly to training and into working hard when they do come. It must be continually made clear to swimmers that top performances will only follow after at least 150 or 200 miles have been covered in the burst of hard training necessary in a one-peak year and that an average of 20 or 25 miles per week should be covered during the period of hardest training. Some top swimmers will do more, some much less, there can be no hard and fast rules. Training log-books should be written up daily by all serious swimmers. To be really systematic and organised about training, the swimmer must keep a year-round, day-by-day record of the type of training, the distances covered, time spent on exercises, details of swimming races, how he feels, etc. A well-kept log-book with weekly totals shown, will allow a good analysis to be made of a swimmer's progress and much can be learned by both swimmer and coach. In 1947 we first insisted on our pupils keeping log-books, so that now some of our present pupils have a detailed record of their training, stretching back ten years or more.

Often Top swimmers will not be able to do *all* that has been planned, but the successful trainer will NOT be too 'easy-going.' He must be a DRIVER and should push his pupils to complete their schedules. Quite often school studies and examinations will make it very difficult for the swimmer to keep up his 20 miles or so per week. However, you will find that there have been breaks in their training if you examine the log-books of even the greatest swimmers. Yet the basic fact remains that it takes 200 miles or more over a period of two or three months for most swimmers to approach top results in a one-peak year. This has been our experience in Australia, and in U.S.A. at the Indiana University, Jim Counsilman, one of the world's most successful coaches, has his boys completing about 600 miles of intensive interval training in a year – they do this in about eleven months of swimming. Four or five of his teenage boys have broken world records in recent years.

In various books and articles you will find *many* detailed schedules for interval training. Some of these are so complicated that I believe they would be impractical when a trainer tried to apply the system to a *group* of swimmers. The system I recomment is a straightforward method of doing interval-type training which can be easily understood and can be carried out by swimmers themselves even without the presence of a trainer. All you need is a minute clock, visible from both ends of the pool, and a reasonably clear stretch of water. An ordinary clock with a minute hand is quite satisfactory for timing if it is big enough to be read easily. For years (since 1946), in Australia our training group at the North Sydney Olympic Pool was alone in its use of a large clock for training, but now there must be thousands of minute-clocks being used in pools all around the world. I believe they are essential for training a group.

The training programme should not be too 'easy' and should always represent a challenge. We write up the daily training for each group on cardboard sheets using waterproof coloured pencils. For individuals these group schedules can be varied, especially for top swimmers. Each week there may be a change in the programme, which usually becomes tougher as the season progresses.

To some extent older sprint swimmers may concentrate more on the shorter distance items, but in general we find that even the sprinters should train with some 400 m swims, and while they are *young* (say up to 14 or 15) *all* swimmers should train as though they were going to be 400 m swimmers. Those with special aptitude will become sprinters in due course but, by their early distance training, they will have developed hearts and lungs to give good endurance. Other things being equal (aptitude, strength, etc.), this endurance capacity will play an important part in making the champion. Practically all of our free-style sprint champions in Australia have started as 400 m and 1,500 m swimmers. Did you know, for example, that Jon Henricks (Olympic 100 m winner in 1956) until the age of 15 was a 1,500 m swimmer and in 1953 won the Australian championship at this distance?

Heart rate counting, as used after the first two swims of the day, will be discussed in detail in Chapter 10. We seldom count heart rates during interval training because I do not believe it is worth the trouble. It is my experience that when the interval training is too severe for him a swimmer will just not keep up, and no harm is done.

With many top swimmers either I, or the swimmers themselves, count the heart rates after each of the two 'effort' swims at the beginning of the training session, but this scientific aid is *not* absolutely essential and may easily be omitted. Too much show of 'science' at the pool side will often waste valuable minutes. There is the correct time and place for scientific observation and research. Many of the ideas presented here as a guide are based on a large amount of scientific observation and experiment, but fundamentally, for success, a trainer needs *practical experience*, knowledge, and above all enthusiasm to drive his swimmers to train hard.

The use of the heart rate counting after the first two swims of the session (the 'efforts') is to enable the trainer and swimmer to assess swimming condition without the necessity of an all-out swim (a 100% effort). All-out races and time-trials for distances above 50 m should generally be restricted to about one a week. Too many races seem to 'deplete' the nervous resources and, I believe, must be avoided. You can read more of this concept later. The 'big' race really should be the only time to attempt to determine what is a swimmer's maximum possible performance. The details of how to make these heart counts and how to interpret the results in relation to the times recorded in the efforts, we shall leave now until Chapter 10.

Efforts

These swims, usually made at the beginning of the training session, are really 'dress-rehearsals' of the race. The swimmer dives in as the minute-hand crosses the zero on the clock and takes note of the time when he finishes. The coach may notice the time after the first 50 m and at the half distance in order to help the pupil in his judgment of pace. Swimmers should learn and practise 'even speed' swimming in these efforts.

A 90% effort, by my definition, is a swim at about 90% of the *speed* of an all-out swim. A swimmer capable of 70 seconds, swimming at 90% should aim to swim with enough output of energy to give him a time approximately one-tenth slower – that is $70 + 7 = 77$ seconds. An 80% effort would be 70 seconds plus *two* tenths of 70, that is $70 + 14 = 84$ seconds, and so on. This idea of training (the repeating of *many* 'effort' swims at the race distance, from 80% to 90%) was introduced to Australian swimmers in the 1940s by the late Professor Frank Cotton.

Interval Training

The term 'interval' training has been used by coaches to describe various ways of combining periods of relatively intense effort with intervals of rest. Some swimmers alternate bursts of fast swimming with recovery periods of much slower swimming or kicking. Theoretically there is a lot to be said for this way, but I found that with large squads it was difficult with this method to keep a close check on what individual swimmers were doing. Thus in recent years we have settled for what might be called *repetition interval training*, where distances from about 15 yards to 440 yards are swum at fairly intense effort with differing periods of rest – from 10 seconds to a minute or so – in between. You will see that nowadays my training system is almost entirely based on the principle of repetition interval training. In the future we shall learn, first, I think, from animal experiments, what is the best way to carry out interval training. Until then we must be content with making educated guesses.

Swimming all Styles

In our School of Swimming at Ryde we work on the idea that after the child has learned to swim 20 yards, about three months of regular practice and teaching should be devoted to his crawl stroke and to making him stronger in the water. Children at this stage come to us four to six times a week for training and instruction in 45 to 60-minute classes. After the first few months of swimming, when the child is able to swim about 100 m with a good crawl stroke, he learns to swim first back-stroke then breast-stroke and butterfly, so that by the middle of a youngster's second season (usually by the age of 9 or 10) all strokes can be swum reasonably well for competition in club races.

When Improver swimmers enter Intermediate groups, we always insist on at least a little of each stroke being done at every training session even though they may now be starting to specialise in one or two strokes. Generally there is a concentration on two styles for which a swimmer shows particular aptitude. Sometimes during the intense training period, if there is evidence of 'staleness' of nervous origin, we change a swimmer for a while almost completely on to his second style. This often proves a very effective means of protecting from further fatigue those parts of the nervous system which are involved in the swimmer's major style.

When swimmers are in hard training they *should* often be very tired. It is a matter of experience to know how hard the coach should 'drive' his pupils before he takes the pressure off. There may be times when swimmers will need a few days or more of either complete rest or relatively easy work.

You will notice that *no* provision has been made for 'warming-up' swims at the beginning of training. The reason for this is *time*. In practice I find that doing some land exercises is sufficient preparation. At Ryde we work for about ten minutes with weights, then after some flexibility exercises we get the swimmers straight into their training without taking up valuable pool space with slow swimming. The 80% effort (the first swim) in the morning session I have found quite slow enough to act as a warm up.

TRAINING FOR TOP OLDER SWIMMERS

We aim for ten or eleven sessions each week. The programme that follows would be for an experienced swimmer in hard training.

Morning Session

Item 1
EFFORTS

Effort swims are generally made at 100 m, 200 m or 400 m. Two effort swims are made, one at 80% then one at 90%, with 2 minutes rest after the first fairly easy, 80% effort. Record the times, and the heart rate response in a special book kept for that purpose, and later in the swimmer's personal log-book. (For details of pulse counting, see later. It is by no means *essential* to count heart rates in order to train effectively.)

Item 2
REPEATS

16 × 100 m or 8 × 200 m or 4 × 400 m leaving respectively every 2, 4 or 7 minutes by the clock. Times may be recorded for future reference. They are made at distinctly *less* than 100% effort – somewhere about 90%. The swimmer stays in the water between swims, while waiting for 'the minute.' Then the coach has time to instruct, making comments on technique, etc.

Item 3
PULLING

In this 'arms only' training, the legs are held together with rubber bands, cut from auto inner tyre tubes. 16 × 50 m or 8 × 100 m or 4 × 200 m pushing off every 1, 2 or 4 minutes by the clock.

Item 4
MEDLEY
SPRINTS

16 × 50 m at all four styles (4 × 50 m of each). Pushing off every minute and every 1½ minutes for breast-stroke.

On alternate days the medley sprints should be carried out before the pulling. When reducing the total distance covered, the pulling or medley sprints can be cut down. Kicking may be substituted for some of the medley sprints.

Afternoon Session

Item 1
PULLING
AND KICKING

It is possible to do this individual type of work in a fairly crowded pool.

At 90%, 4 to 8 × 400 m, alternate pulling and kicking at two or three styles. The 400 m may be timed on the large minute clock. Some kicking may be done either in 400 m time trials or in bursts of 50 m fast – 50 m slowly. Total 1 to 2 miles of this mixed pulling and kicking.

As with the morning programme this may need to be modified for various reasons, e.g. it should allow for extra work on each individual's weakest points. You will notice that kicking is included in this programme although in more advanced swimmers not very much emphasis is placed on it. What kicking is done should mostly be at a high tempo, concentrating on looseness and flexibility of knee and ankle joints. Personally I think it is better to concentrate on the flick *downwards* of the feet, rather than the up-beat (which was popularised by Jean Taris in the early 1930s). The best type of leg kick will vary with individuals. It may be that equal stress should be placed on both up and down beats. It is paradoxical that many great crawl swimmers appear to use a 'normal,' continuous six-beat leg kick in kick-board practice, but use a different, 'broken-tempo' action when the legs are combined with arms in the full stroke. More of this in the chapters on the crawl stroke.

Item 2
SPRINTS

Short sprints at all styles, with only short rests between them.

A total distance of from 800 m to 1,500 m made up of sprints of 25 m or even 12 m or so (if the swims must be done *across* the pool). When made across the pool two laps can be swum. Depending on the distance of the sprints the swimmers should leave every 30 seconds or 20 seconds by the minute clock. The coach will be able to remind swimmers of points of technique between sprints.

The programme here can be quite flexible. The coach might first require (in the 25 m pool) 32 × 25 m crawl-stroke sprints pushing off every 30 seconds. Then he might ask for 4 × 25 m at butterfly, back-stroke, breast-stroke and crawl – every 45 seconds. Another item may be 'doubles' 8 × 2 laps, concentrating on 'tumble' turns. At this stage there might be a special lesson on 'tumbling' with individual practice. Finally the sprint programme may conclude with 16 × 25 m sprints leaving every 30 seconds. Of course this programme must be varied accordingly if the sprints must be done at shorter distances across the pool. The sprints, and other training, must often be carried out by dividing swimmers into two or three groups leaving on whistle blasts at intervals of about 10 seconds.

TRAINING PROGRAMME FOR YOUNG TOP SWIMMERS
Morning Session

Item 1
EFFORTS

4 × 100 m or 2 × 400 m or 800 m. *Not* 'all-out,' but at about 90%. Record times in book. Rest for say 3 minutes between efforts.

Item 2
REPEATS

16 × 50 m pushing off every minute by the clock or 8 × 100 m every 2 minutes. (On every 2½ minutes for other than crawl stroke.)

Item 3
PULLING

16 × 50 m leaving every 1½ minutes or 8 × 100 m leaving every 2½ minutes.

Item 4
MEDLEY
SPRINTS

4 × 50 m breast-stroke every 1½ minutes.
4 × 50 m back-stroke every 1½ minutes.
4 × 50 m butterfly every 1½ minutes.
4 × 50 m crawl every 1 minute.

Afternoon Session

PULLING AND   Pulling and kicking, exactly as for older swimmers,
KICKING   even up to 8 × 400 m pulling and kicking at
               various styles.
               This is followed by ½ to 1 mile of short sprints
               (12 m to 25 m), as for older swimmers.

TRAINING PROGRAMME FOR INTERMEDIATE SWIMMERS

For those of all ages not up to the standard of 'Top Younger
Swimmers' but able to swim at least 200 m without stopping.

Morning Session

Item 1   Two 100 m or 200 m efforts. Each swimmer takes
EFFORTS   his own time from the pool minute-clock and
                writes it down in the coach's book.

Item 2   8 × 50 m crawl-stroke leaving every 1½ minutes by
REPEATS   the clock. Several groups of pupils, each group of
                a similar standard, can work together for this
                training with 10 seconds between each group.
                4 × 50 m back-stroke every 1½ minutes.
                4 × 50 m breast-stroke every 2 minutes.
                (Butterfly stroke is carried out in afternoon
                training.)

Item 3   8 × 50 m with legs tied.
PULLING   Trainer can decide what styles should be used for
                various individuals. This training often has to be
                done independently by swimmers. They are told to
                rest 10 seconds at end of each 50 m.

Item 4   8 × 50 m kicking sprints (sometimes without
KICKING   board), with 20 second rests between sprints.

Item 5
LONG SLOW   400 m at only 75%, but without stopping.
SWIM

Afternoon Session

                In general the same programme is given as for the
                Top Younger Swimmers. This programme can be
                made easier in the following way:

Item 1   4 to 8 × 200 m made up as follows:
PULLING AND   1 × 200 m crawl-stroke pulling
KICKING   1 × 200 m crawl-stroke kicking
                1 × 200 m breast-stroke pulling

1 × 200 m breast-stroke kicking
1 × 200 m back-stroke pulling
1 × 200 m back-stroke kicking

These swims may or may not be timed depending on the opportunity to do this. The important thing is to get the miles done *with attention to good technique.*

Item 2
SPRINTS

Short sprints as for Top Younger Swimmers, but over a smaller total distance of 400 m to 800 m. Each sprint can be done over a very short distance, even 10 m or so. Butterfly stroke can be taught during these sprint periods.

We find that these sprints can provide a very good place for teaching technique, for teaching turns, starts and finishes, and for practising swimming on the one breath necessary for sprint racing. Particularly with these younger children it is best if the trainer can supervise these sprints carefully rather than tell the children to push off and swim 'every 30 seconds.'

Item 3
LONG SLOW
SWIM

Finish off with a 'long' easy swim at about 75% effort, 200 m or 400 m without stopping.

As I have already indicated these training schedules are offered as a guide, not to be copied slavishly in every detail. If you came any day to the Ryde Pool you would *not* see us sticking rigidly to every detail of these programmes. We make week-by-week and day-by-day variations in each item.

No doubt better programmes will be devised and we shall modify somewhat our training routines in the future, but this type of training *has* produced a number of swimmers with world class times, and even in the week that I write these words we have had three 15-year-old boys with swims under 59 seconds for the 110 yards and under 4-30 seconds for the 440 yards. Four 15-year-olds made an Australian record of 3 minutes 55.0 seconds for 4 × 110 yards relay in long course, a 15-year-old girl did 1 minute 21.4 seconds for 110 yards breast-stroke and a 12-year-old girl won the 110 yards under-16 Australian Championship for butterfly-stroke in 1 minute 13.6 seconds.

These schedules are too much for some swimmers. Observation of the individual, and experience, will teach the coach that not everyone can 'take' really hard training, although to produce outstanding results many miles must be covered in the year – as a rough guide between 200 and 600 miles. The good coach will make less mistakes in judgment of his pupil's capacity for hard work than will the inexperienced novice.

Those who believe that the secret of superior swimming is 'just a tremendous amount of hard work' may be misguided. Hard work – as hard as the individual can carry – *is* certainly important, but it is quite possible to 'go stale' because the sum total of stresses, including training, which are acting on the individual, is too great.

We take up the problem of over-training in more detail in Part 2 – The Science of Training.

Now the very important consideration – how to reach a peak for important races.

CHAPTER THREE

How to Reach a Peak

FOR reasons that will soon become clear we call the final preparation for the big race the *tapering-off period*.

The final goal and the ultimate problem facing any coach is to bring the swimmer to his peak for a particular race after a period of hard training. The trainer's ambition should be to have all of his pupils swim their personal best times (or close to them) in the big races. The programme and general instructions which follow are the result of our observations and study of this problem.

As with training schedules, there are many factors influencing the situation, so the plan of tapering-off suggested here should never be applied *too* rigidly. We use this as a basis but sometimes vary it considerably for individual swimmers.

The important *principle* is that after a strenuous two or three months of training there should be a very distinct easing of hard training and an introduction of more rest starting from about *three weeks before important events*, although for events of less importance swimmers often need not break their routine of hard training for more than one to four days before the race, when they can take up the last part of the tapering-off programme. Of course this long taper-off applies to swimmers who have been in really hard training for several months. If the hard training has not been done there can hardly be top performances anyway. The less training, the less need for tapering-off. I remember in 1947 sitting with the late Professor Frank Cotton ('father' of scientific training in Australia) and working out a final preparation programme. Professor Cotton and I pondered for a long time on what to call this programme and finally hit upon a term which well describes the process of doing gradually less hard training – 'tapering-off.' The name has stuck.

Individuals differ in the amount of easing-off from hard

Murray Rose (Australia), the only swimmer ever to win the Olympic 400 metres event twice. Murray illustrates well, characteristics in technique which have distinguished the modern Australian crawlstroke – the roll of the body around the longitudinal axis and the use of shoulders and back in the pull.

At Ryde we are proud of these four boys who at fifteen years of age were all Australian junior champions in 1963. Together the four made the National Junior 4 × 110 yards relay record in the excellent time of 3 minutes 55 seconds, an average of under 59 seconds for each swimmer. Peter Bryant's official split time in this relay swim was 57.4 seconds. *Left to right:* John Pick; his best performances as a 15-year-old, 440 yards freestyle 4 minutes 28.7 seconds, and 1,650 yards 17 minutes 45.5 seconds. Peter Bryant; National Junior champion 110 and 440 yards. Russell Phegan; National Junior 220 yards champion – best 220 yards 2 minutes 6.7 seconds – best 440 yards 4 minutes 28.5 seconds – best 880 yards 9 minutes 14.1 seconds. Les Trengove; at 15 swam the 110 in 60 seconds flat and *ran* the 100 yards track in 10.1 seconds. He also swam 110 yards 'Jastremski style' breaststroke in 1 minute 17 seconds.

Notice the excellent muscular development, especially of the upper bodies. These boys have exercised strenuously with weights during the off-season for at least four years. Early in 1964 Russell Phegan at 16 years of age became one of the fastest ever 400 metres swimmers with 4 minutes 17.9 seconds.

training that they need. We have found that sprint swimmers (100 m and 200 m) who tend to be more 'highly strung' need more rest than distance performers. Younger swimmers, we find, need less easing-off than older swimmers.

The following programme should serve as an *indication* of the type of tapering to be carried out after about three months of very hard training. We have found, as I have stressed, that rarely would any swimmer do *exactly* what is on this programme because some changes will always have to be made to meet varying circumstances.

A TAPERING-OFF PROGRAMME

From Week 4 to Week 3 Before Important Event

This is the final period of very strenuous training (four to six miles per day). A final burst of hard interval-type training should be made during this week, perhaps 25 miles during the week.

From Week 3 to Week 2

This should be a relatively easy week to allow general recuperation of the body from the very strenuous training. Although it is a good idea to keep up the usual routine of coming to the pool twice a day (or at least once), the swimming during this week should be quite easy 'basic swimming,' (about 75% of race speed) and the daily training distance is cut down to around two miles. You may do about 400 m of interval training.

Make one time-trial at the end of this week under as good pool conditions as possible. If the time is very bad (say more than about 5% worse than the swimmer's best time for the distance) then maintain a similar, very easy programme for yet another week. A poor time generally indicates that the swimmer needs *more* rest. Do not make the all too common mistake of training *harder* when performances are bad at this stage. A poor performance here shows that the body has not recuperated from the earlier hard training, but we have found that for swimmers even in a state of chronic fatigue, three or four weeks *easy* swimming will usually bring them to near top performances, provided, of course that there have been 200 miles or so of hard training carried out in the previous two or three months. No swimmer can hope to do his personal best time without the background of solid training in the water.

B

From Week 2 to Week 1

If the time-trial or race at the end of Week 3 is reasonably good, the swimmer may increase his training again and start the time-honoured 'sharpening up' with more sprints. But it is still much better to *under-train* than to risk doing too much at any time during these few weeks before the big race. Here is the kind of programme the swimmer may carry out in two sessions a day from Week 2 to Week 1.

Morning   Exercises (5 to 10 minutes including some with weights)

Easy 400 m (75% race speed)

Race distance (80% race speed)

Race distance (90% race speed)

Race distance (80% race speed)

Walk-backs. 8 × 50 m walking back to start in 50 m pool, with 1 or 2 minutes rest between sprints (each 50 m at 95%)

Easy 400 m (75%)

Afternoon   Exercises (5 to 10 minutes, some with weights)

Easy 400 m (75%)

Short sprints (400 m to 800 m of 15 m to 25 m swims). Usually across pool

Easy 400 m (75%)

Some swimmers find it best to omit the second swimming session. We often train swimmers only once a day at this stage but strong swimmers, particularly distance swimmers in good form, can carry out the two sessions.

One Week Before Big Races

Swim once per day only

Easy 400 m (75% of race speed)

Race distance at 80% of race speed

Race distance at 90% of race speed

'Under distance' at 95%. Swim three-quarters of race distance at fast speed

Walk-backs. 8 × 50 m with 1 to 2 minutes rest between each 50 m. Swim at 95% effort.

This training should be reduced a little each day. Remember that over-training during this period will prevent a swimmer reaching a high peak in performance. Again I emphasise that it

is better to DO TOO LITTLE rather than too much at this stage, and
it is important to get plenty of rest.

Day Before Race

Either no swimming, or 800 m of easy swimming only.We do
not want a session of interval training on this day. It surprises
me to see rival coaches, sometimes with stop-watches out,
urging their pupils to swim fast times the day before an important contest. Better the good time in the race!

On Day of Race

The 'rested' body has now to be made ready for the big effort.
Rise late in the morning and from then on become active. Four
to six hours before the race go to the competition pool or, if
this is not possible, try to go to another pool, and do –
Exercises (5 to 10 minutes)
400 m slowly (75% of race speed)
Then 100 m, or 200 m at 90% to 95% effort (this is the
     'wake-up' swim)
Two or three starts and short sprints
200 m slowly (75%)

Food Before the Race

The principle to be followed is to eat a fairly light, easily
digested meal at least three hours before the race. So that it can
pass quickly through the stomach this meal may be in a semi-
liquid form. Nowadays there are on the market in many
countries several types of such semi-liquid pre-race meals which
will prove particularly useful for those competitors who suffer
from 'nervous stomach' on the race day. Fats and proteins are
slowly digested and during strong emotional tension can remain
in the stomach for hours. Carbohydrates are more easily
digested and, being more readily used for fuel by the active
muscles, make the best pre-race meal. To prevent feelings of
hunger before the race you may suck glucose sweets.

Body Weight

Swimmers should take great care not to increase their body
weight during the three-week easing-off period because I believe
that fat laid down in the muscles will impair their physical effi-

ciency. With less training than usual, and more free time, swimmers are inclined to over-eat, whereas the ideal situation is to lose a pound or two during the tapering period.

At International contests swimmers must eat sparingly despite the temptations of plentiful and interesting foods, if they want to represent their country well and perform their best. I have seen swimmers of many nations over-eat and become fat and sluggish at Olympic Games.

Shaving the Skin Smooth

About one week before important races the legs and arms (and in the case of men, the chest) should be shaved smooth to cut down water resistance. Australian Jon Henricks in 1955 was one of the first world-class swimmers to do this, but now it is common practice with all Australian and most American and Dutch top swimmers. I have seen the results of tests which indicate that shaving may make even 1 to 2 seconds difference in 100 m and that the effect is probably *more* than merely psychological.

Take great care when shaving that you do not remove skin! Use an electric razor and work slowly but thoroughly. Shave about a week before an important race to get used to the feel of it, and then shave again about two days before, with possibly a final touching up on the morning of the race.

Auto-Suggestion

In the future, I have no doubt it will be proved that certain mental processes will greatly help race performance. The power of the psychological process of suggestion is great, and so is auto- (or self) suggestion which any swimmer can carry out for himself regularly.

In your 'mind's eye,' just before sleeping at night or while relaxing, 'see' yourself and 'feel' yourself swimming as you want to. Mentally practice and visualise your stroke, your turn, your start. 'See' and 'feel' yourself swimming well, and unconsciously your body *will bring about the idea*. In this way the power of suggestion will help you. I earnestly advise you to carry this procedure out regularly. Do not allow negative harmful ideas (such as 'I can't win,' etc.) to fill your mind. Just before, and in the race itself, concentrate on positive, helpful thoughts such as

'This is easy, the further I go, the easier it becomes.' At the pool, as the race time gets closer, think of the high tempo and power of your stroking, good judgment of lap-pace, etc. Feel certain that you *will* turn well. Do not waste your mental energy worrying about *other* competitors or about failure. Your job is to get the utmost out of yourself and this takes full concentration. Think *positive* helpful thoughts, not negative harmful ones.

Before Race Warm-up

You have probably noticed that it is not at all unusual for a swimmer's *second* race in a competition to be his fastest. This is a warming-up effect which we can use by making a fairly hard preliminary swim.

About three-quarters of an hour before the first event at a swimming meeting carry out the following:

Exercises (15 minutes)

200 m slowly (75%)

50 m sprint at about 100%

3 × 25 m sprints all-out

100 m slowly

Then if possible take a *hot shower or hot bath* for 6 to 7 minutes followed by a light massage.

If the conditions are very cold in an outdoor pool it is sometimes best not to go into the water before the race but to carry out all the other warming-up activities.

It is an advantage for the body temperature to be raised before racing. For this a hot shower or hot bath should be used either at home before going to the pool or at the pool, or in both places. The water should be just about as hot as the swimmer can bear, then thorough warming up (enough to cause sweating) needs about five minutes in the bath or seven minutes under the shower. The hot water treatment should be followed by a short cold shower to close the skin blood-vessels. The hot shower at the pool should be taken after the pre-race swim. In 1947 we carried out a series of careful scientific experiments (over 400 individual swims were involved) which proved that this 'passive' warming-up was helpful. If you are interested in reading the details of this experiment see page 143 of *The Research Quarterly*, Volume 27, 1956.

While waiting for the race, be sure to put on warm clothes and cover the feet. The swimmer should alternate between lying down (have a rug and if possible a mattress) and walking around and exercising. Our experiments showed that even in a warm atmosphere, if a swimmer is immobile for a while, isolated muscles can become cold, actually falling to 2 or 3 centigrade degrees below the blood temperature. This can greatly lower the work capacity of the muscle. Exercising the muscles and running from time to time will keep the muscles warm. In Australia I insist on my pupils *running* as part of their warm-up, either up and down the corridors of the pool or where possible outside on the grass. Do not sit still for long. Keep moving! Keep warm!

Massage

On the basis of my own observations I believe that massage is valuable to the sportsman and where practicable arrange for my swimmers to have it.

Nervousness Before the Race

It is good to be nervous and 'keyed-up' before the race because in this state your body can perform better. When you are nervous adrenaline is secreted from your adrenal glands into your bloodstream and it acts on the muscles and on blood capillaries, preparing the body for 'fight and flight,' and thus for greater speed. Some of the best swimmers I have trained have told me they have been very nervous before a big race. One record-breaker told me he could feel his fingers 'tingling.'

Over-Breathing

As you are being called to the starting board, begin breathing more deeply and faster than usual, so that by the time you are on the starting block you will have taken about ten or twelve deep and fast breaths.

This is particularly valuable for the sprinter who must swim much of the race 'on the one breath' so that he can 'fix' his shoulders as firmly as possible, and keep the head low and body horizontal and streamlined.

Even-Pace Swimming

Long before the swimmer gets into top competition he should have learned to judge his speed. Allowing for the dive, he must learn to swim nearly at even speed throughout. This means that he must learn to restrain himself early in the race, particularly in the first 50 m. Many a swimmer has thrown away his chance of success by going too fast early in the race and trying to go to an early lead. There are strong indications now that future record-breaking performances will be made by swimmers who cover the second half of the race distance even faster than the first. In particular be careful of the *first* 50 m because here the greatest damage can be done. A yard or two is very little to make up by a swimmer who has judged his speed well. Making a big effort to keep in front of a much superior rival in the first half of a race, where it means you are not able to swim at an even speed throughout, will result in a slower time than your best. Swimmers must learn to swim their own races. To keep the speed constant you must gradually make a greater and greater effort throughout the race. This means concentration on yourself, not on what your rivals are doing.

Qualifying Heats

Where it is necessary to qualify through heats for a final, swimmers uncertain of reaching the top seven or eight times must of course swim all-out (100%). Swimmers who are obviously capable of quite easily qualifying should swim at between 95% and 99% effort. The qualifying time should seldom be as fast as the time made in a final. The final is when you should make your 100% effort.

Finishing

In crawl-stroke try to touch the wall with one arm stretched out *under* the water. Once you have touched, *stop*. Do not bring the other arm to the wall because some judges will take this as the finishing arm and you may lose in a close race. Good finish-touching takes practice and, like good turning, is one of the techniques which must be learned in training. The problem to be solved in a split-second at the end of every race, is whether to stretch an arm out and kick in to the wall or to take another short stroke. The same problem arises at the finish with each style, whether to stretch out or take another stroke. The result of the race may well rest on your decision. Practise finishing.

Immediately After the Race

To recover quickly after a race the best physiological procedure is to keep exercising – do not stay still. Even while waiting for others to finish the race you can move around a little in the water. At the appropriate time you can push off and swim half way up the lap, then back again. At the Rome Olympics the Americans very wisely swam two laps of the pool! When you come out of the water keep the muscles active with exercises and walking, then you will be much fitter for the next race on the same or even the next day. If you have another race that day take great care to keep warm and exercise continually as described in the warming-up instructions.

See Your Coach

You should arrive at the pool about 45 minutes before the first race is timed to start, and report near the starting blocks to your coach before your preliminary swim. If possible just before you go down to report for the start of your race, see him again. Soon after the race you should report once again to discuss your performance whilst it is fresh in mind. As soon as you come out of the water after your race politely ask the three time-takers behind your lane for your time. Quite often they will tell you, but of course sometimes they will not.

Sportsmanship

It is easy to be a good sport when you *win* but more difficult when you don't. If you don't do well, be determined to do better next time, but *do not offer excuses*. Nobody is really interested in your troubles and excuses. You must train yourself to accept victory calmly and modestly, and defeat without bitterness. If you cannot learn to 'take' defeats and disappointments you will soon worry yourself out of swimming, so in the long run an attitude of good sportsmanship means survival in swimming. Particularly in the case of younger swimmers the attitude of the parents in regard to sportsmanship can have an important effect on the child. In swimming, as in life, nobody can go on winning *all* the time – there will always be success modified by some disappointments. The important thing is to keep on striving to do better next time.

CHAPTER FOUR

More on Race Preparation

IN my first summer in Holland as Dutch National coach in 1962 the greatest problems were first to get the top swimmers to work hard enough at interval training, and *then* once they were training well, to prevent them from swimming too hard in the final two weeks or so before the European Championships in Leipzig. In order to explain the scientific basis for tapering-off I wrote an article for swimmers and coaches in *Zwemkroniek*, the Dutch swimming magazine published every week in the Netherlands.

Here is the article, entitled 'Reaching a Peak for Leipzig.'

'Many swimmers and trainers do not yet understand fully the fundamental concepts involved in training to reach a peak performance. Let me try to make these points clearer. The best possible training for a peak performance requires much more than natural ability in the swimmer and "plenty of hard swimming." Hard training is the first rough approach to reaching top performance but there is rather more to it than this alone.

'I have pointed out before in *Zwemkroniek* that the great majority of Australian swimmers have for the past ten years or so managed to reach their peak performances at their National Championships and at the Olympic Games. This has not happened by chance but generally as the result of a planned programme of hard work, and then rest. *Both* are equally important in reaching a peak. Swimmers, of course, react in an individual way and now and then we get surprises, and performances occur which we find difficult to explain. It is, nevertheless, possible to formulate some general principles which should be understood well by every swimmer, coach and official.

'With the constant stress of hard training, the body gradually adapts itself for top performance. In recent years we have found that the stress must be great (much greater than was previously thought possible) and that nearly all of the present top swimmers in the U.S.A. and Australia had started their hard training by the time they were twelve years of age or so. Further, it has been clearly demonstrated that the general conditioning method known as Interval Training is more successful than those which consist mainly of swimming long distances at moderate speed. Exercise, besides training the circulatory and respiratory systems, also involves the use of particular 'motor' nerve cells in the brain and nervous pathways.

'It is possible for the respiratory and circulatory systems (lungs, heart, blood vessels) to be well adapted for top performance and show no sign of strain, but it appears that at the same time *specific parts of the nervous system may be fatigued.* When this occurs physiological tests of fitness (electrocardiograph, blood pressure responses etc.) will often be normal, yet performances in swimming races will be bad. Excellent demonstration of the truth of this theory of 'nervous depletion' is given by the common observation that a swimmer training hard for say the crawl-stroke may be making bad times, but on changing over to his second style, the swimmer comes up with a personal best performance. The parts of the nervous system involved in the crawl action appear to be temporarily worn out, but the cells and nerve pathways involved in making the complex actions of the second stroke remain unfatigued, and performance here is relatively good. There is good experimental evidence that severe exertion can in some way "deplete" the nervous system. Severely exercised experimental rats lose the Nissyl granules which are found in the nerve cells of rested rats.

'It is not a great step to apply the implications of this knowledge to the training of sportsmen and, in particular, swimmers. A proper understanding of the principle of Nervous Reserve will influence greatly the way in which swimmers undertake their final preparation for an important event. Some swimmers are able to train very hard (four to six miles per day of interval training) and will still improve in their weekly time trials. Others improve for a few weeks and then appear to be getting no faster. What is happening is that *potentially* the swimmer is improving, but his nervous system is becoming fatigued. We have demonstrated with laboratory tests that there is a week-by-week increase in physiological fitness during training but it seems that this is always balanced by some degree of nervous depletion. Within reason the swimmer whose times are not improving should in most circumstances continue training hard UNLESS he or she is within three weeks of a big contest. If performances at time trials are bad three weeks before the important event then it is looking for trouble not to ease down the training. This has been my repeated experience with swimmers for twenty years. If a particular swimmer with a great capacity for absorbing large amounts of training improves in performance week by week and never becomes very fatigued, then this lucky individual may train quite hard up to a week or so before his big race. However, at that stage, in order to do his best, even he should ease up.

'Note that in general I do *not* suggest doing nothing at all when performances are bad. Rather than complete rest, I usually suggest less intense swimming (basic swimming at 75%).

'The fitness of respiratory and circulatory systems appears to be held for a week or two after hard training is eased off, so a swimmer who has trained hard need not be afraid of doing less swimming for a while. It is on this point that I find swimmers, trainers, and parents need to be continually reassured. The swimmer who feels that he *must* be training very hard close to an important contest, as far as swimming knowledge is concerned, is still a child.'

'Occasionally, in the course of a swimmer's preparation, when his body is adapting well and sometimes just before the nervous factor finally "cracks," there may be excellent performances. Then the swimmer, coach and parents will often argue in this way: "Hard training gave a good performance, so if performance is bad, then *more* hard training must be done to swim fast again." It is a trap that so many swimmers and coaches have fallen into and are still falling into all over the world. Some swimmers and coaches do not have the knowledge, or the confidence, to ease-up sufficiently. Many just keep on going, swimming hard and committing swimming "suicide."

'Nearly every top swimmer will quite often be trained to the point of nervous fatigue. If the coach reacts properly all will be well, but if he or the swimmer responds by driving on with hard training, often all will be lost. On occasions a week or more of complete rest, out of the water, should be taken even during the final preparation for a big event, but usually the programme should be greatly eased down to include only slow swimming once a day with perhaps one or two complete days' rest each week.

'I have often talked to former swimmers about this question of tapering-off training and of resting before the big race. Many have recalled from their own experience occasions when they were prevented by various circumstances from swimming at all for a week or so before a race. In one case it was because of travel by ship, in another it was because of being in hospital with a stomach disorder – but the result was the same – personal best performances and often records following the enforced period of rest.

'I give notice here to members of the Dutch National team, that within a week or so of International contests, I shall be using the "rest principle" very much more than the "train hard" principle. My experience as coach has convinced me of the great importance of the "rest principle" in making peak performances.

'Finally let me tell you a short story.

'At the 1952 Olympic Games at Helsinki there was an Australian swimmer, John Davies, the butterfly breast-stroker (butterfly with the arms, and breast-stroke with the leg kick was allowed then). A week before the qualifying heats he swam very slowly in a time-trial, finishing exhausted. He was clearly over-trained. From then on we only permitted him to swim slowly about 800 m in one training session each day. Then for three days before his qualifying heat he spent 20 hours each day in his bed sleeping. In these three days he *did not swim at all.*

'The result? the records of the Olympic Games will tell you. First place – John G. Davies (Australia) and his time, an Olympic record (and his personal best-ever).

'My experience with John Davies illustrates the principle that it is better, far better, to rest too much than to train too much and too hard in final preparation. The over-trained, over-tired swimmer has *no* chance. There is no knowing what the fresh, well-rested swimmer may do with the stimulus of the great excitement of International competition. If a swimmer is over-trained the results can be disastrous. They can be monumental flops.

'In Leipzig, we want fresh, well-rested swimmers representing the Netherlands.'

During the summer of 1962 the performances of the Dutch swimmers had not been very encouraging. The sports writers in Holland were not slow in pointing this out and predicting failure. Quite frankly we were all worried. However, as things turned out the gloom was not justified. The Dutch girls swept nearly all before them at Leipzig, placing their two entries in the first four in every swimming event, and they won the Braedius Cup for European swimming supremacy. Their times by and large were only a shade behind the outstanding American girls. The Dutch men in the whole history of European championships had previously won just one medal, but at Leipzig they made their mark when Johan Bontekoe won the Men's 400 m, and in all they won five swimming medals. There were Dutch finalists in every swimming event except one.

Perhaps more important than the number of medals gained was the fact that every one of the twenty-two in the Dutch National team recorded their best times of the summer at the

championships, and twenty made their personal best-ever times.
European coaches and the Press were very interested in *why*
the Dutch suddenly made such good times. It was even suggested that I had hypnotised the swimmers or that we had used
an effective 'pep pill'!

There were several factors contributing to the Dutch success;
not the least, of course, was the ability of the swimmers. Also,
due to the excellent leadership from the male and female officials,
we had a particularly well-disciplined and happy team. Much of
the credit for the success of this 1962 Dutch National team must
go to these officials, who helped me ensure that the team was
well tapered-off and well rested.

You might like to know just what the team did in the final
stages of its preparation.

Here are the *exact* instructions that were handed out to the
team members eight days before the championships when they
came together for a short training camp at Borne in East Holland
before travelling to Leipzig in East Germany.

What the Dutch swimmers did before Leipzig is the same
basic preparation that we do with all our pupils before top
competition.

INSTRUCTIONS TO DUTCH TEAM FOR LEIPZIG

The standard in Europe today is higher than ever and we are *not*
expected to do well. We cannot leave anything to chance. We must
use all the science and experience available to us to reach peak
performances.

Collectively there have been about eighteen trainers involved in
training members of this team. The KNZB (Royal Dutch Swimming
Association) has appointed me to represent these trainers here and at
Leipzig. I must ask every swimmer for his full co-operation and help.
Handling the training of twenty-two team members is not easy for
one person but under European conditions most countries find that
they must appoint *one* coach to be in full charge for the final week or
so before the competition.

Training From Now
*From now on you must all start storing up nervous energy and do
only just enough swimming to hold your condition.* Even if some of you
did not swim at all for about a week before your race at Leipzig, you
would swim close to your fastest times. We must be careful to do too

little, rather than too much. From now on you must get plenty of sleep and rest.

Your training sessions during Week 2 to Week 1 before Leipzig will in general consist of the items which follow. How much you do of each item will depend on various circumstances such as the exact day of your first race in Leipzig, etc.

Item 1. Exercises (warming up and flexibility). To be demon-strated.

Item 2. Some slow, warm-up swimming 400 m or 800 m.

Item 3. Sometimes, ONE swim at race distance (or less) at no more than 90%.

Item 4. Sprints, four to eight, 50 m with 1 to 2 minute rests.

Item 5. A few starts, and relay change-overs.

Item 6. Slow swimming (200 m) to finish off.

The above basic programme will be used, with variations for individuals, both now (the week before Leipzig) and also at Leipzig.

I shall usually be quite happy to allow team members to do *less* than the amount set out above (and even to miss out on training sessions if you feel you need more rest). Only in exceptional circumstances can swimmers be permitted to train any harder. From now on, no swims more than 50 m should be at '100% effort' until your first big race at Leipzig.

If some swimmers desire to vary greatly the above programme I would like them to come and see me as soon as possible so that we can talk things over.

At Leipzig

For two or three days before racing I want each Dutch swimmer to swim easily (about 400 m or 800 m) with possibly one or two 50 m sprints. On the day of your races we shall be sure that you warm-up thoroughly with swimming and *exercises*. When you have a race either at a 10 a.m. or a 4 p.m. session I want each swimmer to report to me at the starting end of the pool at 9.15 a.m. or 3.15 p.m. Have warm clothes on under your track suits. We shall make sure you exercise and do some quite vigorous swimming. Then will follow a light massage.

Just before your massage, even though you may never have done this before, I advise you strongly to take a warm shower (followed by a short cold shower). After the massage you should *keep moving*. Put on warm clothes and do not sit down for more than a few minutes at a time. Do loosening-up exercises and walk around (with an occasional short run).

Just before the start take six to twelve deep breaths. As you are called to 'take your marks' you should be breathing deeply.

I do not intend to try changing any swimmer's stroking techniques at this stage *but* I do want you to take up positions on the starting blocks which do not cause you to fall into the water before the gun. Remember in the start you should have your arms in such a position that the *first movement* with them is a *vigorous thrust* backwards. This helps to drive the body forwards.

I know that many of you in the Netherlands have had to train in crowded pools and in outdoor pools where the water was far from being clear, but at Leipzig you will have clear water and a black line to guide you. This means that you can keep your heads down and know where you are going. Starting here at Borne, eight days before the European championships, and in your training at Leipzig, concentrate on *not* lifting the head to look where you are going or to look at your rivals, which costs you at least a few inches every time (and this you cannot afford to give away). We don't want to see Dutch swimmers wasting their energy looking at rivals, you have enough to think about in getting a 100% effort from yourself.

In training, practice your touching at the finish. Stretching out at the right time (usually touching under water) can save up to half a second in your race time.

Turning: In practice and in your races turn quickly *without* looking at your rivals, and always push off hard.

Shaving the skin: I want all Dutch swimmers to have their legs shaved (and the men their chests as well). This may be worth one or two seconds in every 100 m.

Body weight: During this easing-off period you must not put on weight. This means eating less than during your hard training periods. This is very important. It is up to each individual to do the right thing.

Even laps at Leipzig: Allowing for the two or three seconds due to the start, including the first lap, I want to see good pace judgment at Leipzig by all Dutch swimmers. This means that nearly all of you must hold back more over the first lap, indeed for the first half of your races. There is no prize for being first to turn at the half-way mark. In the first 50 m or 100 m the 'damage' can be done and a good performance spoiled by going too fast early. After the first part of the race, where it does not matter if you are a few metres behind, then gradually put out more and more effort, so that you are trying your utmost in the final lap. This principle of *even* speed swimming has been well and truly proved, so allow yourself to perform your best. The early leader seldom wins big races. Even in top competition I notice all over the world that most competitors make too much effort early in the race. Let *others* make this mistake, but not Dutch swimmers.

Final point: Right thinking: Certain mental processes can improve your race performance. From time to time in your mind's eye, *see* yourself and *feel* yourself swimming just as you want to. I earnestly advise you from now on to carry out this auto-suggestion practice two or three times a day.

Concentrate on this thought – THAT YOU WILL DO WELL IN YOUR BIG RACE.

We can't know for certain how much the instructions did help the Dutch team but I believe that if the ideas were not fairly close to the mark the swimmers could hardly have met with the success they did.

As with the Training Schedules in Chapter 3, please do not take this as the 'last word' on race preparation. We shall continue to learn a little more every year. We must be ready to re-assess and modify our ideas as our knowledge and experience expand.

CHAPTER FIVE

Exercises

STRENGTH and flexibility are very important factors for the competitive swimmer and both can be improved with special exercises. When we speak of flexibility we refer to the degree of mobility of the joints. For swimmers we are particularly concerned with the flexibility of the shoulders and ankles.

Many Dutch coaches during 1962 said this to me: 'We get condition only in the water, we don't want to slow swimmers down by getting them "muscle-bound" with exercises for strength.' On the face of it, this has seemed a good reason in the past for exercising *only* in the water to gain swimming fitness. Up to 1948 practically every swimming trainer in the world agreed with this. Now, however, practical experience has proved them wrong and there are few top swimmers in the world who do *not* work for strength out of the water in addition to their strenuous training in the water.

There is not space here to go fully into the history and theory of strengthening exercises for swimmers, but it might be mentioned that Coach Robert Kiphuth at Yale University (U.S.A.) had been using wall pulley-weights and other exercises for many years before the idea of training with bar-bells was tried by swimmers (one or two Americans but at first mainly Australians). In 1950 when the late John Marshall went from Australia to train under Kiphuth at Yale his best 400 m time was 4 minutes 47 seconds. After a strenuous six months of strengthening exercises John swam a world record of 4 minutes 26.9 seconds. I still have a letter he sent me at that time in which he says he believed that his great improvement was mainly due to the fact that he had increased his body strength by the use of various calisthenic exercises and pulley-weights.

Amongst the first great swimmers to train with iron weights were the outstanding American sprinter Dick Cleveland and the

Australians Dawn Frazer, Jon Henricks and John Konrads. In recent years nearly all the outstanding Australian swimmers have strengthened themselves with weight training. They did *not* become 'muscle-bound,' but they *did* increase the strength of the muscles of their upper bodies (shoulders, back muscles and arms), and they *did* break world records.

After 1956 the majority of American swimmers started serious weight training and now we find that at Indiana University, Jim Counsilman's group of swimmers carry out some weight training all the year, even right up to the day of an important competition, as do my pupils in Sydney.

It is important to *keep* the muscles strong and swimming alone is apparently not enough. The Navy team in the U.S.A. had their most successful season ever during 1961, *after* they had introduced regular weight training. Be assured that the principle of strengthening the swimmer with weights for better performance has been proved now by practical experience.

Strengthening should be done by young swimmers as well as by top swimmers, and weight training and pulley-weight exercises may often have to be carried out in an individual way at home. There may be difficulties in procuring apparatus but 'where there's a will there's a way.' Any individual, even without a trainer, if he is enthusiastic and determined can improve himself greatly by doing exercises regularly, at home or in a class.

Hundreds of strengthening exercises have been suggested for swimmers. We can't give you all of these, but have selected some of the best. In general we have concentrated on those exercises which more or less copy the action made in swimming but which provide greater resistance than in swimming. Because we want to develop and strengthen to some extent all the muscles of the upper body we do not *always* follow rigidly the principle of specific exercises for the swimming muscles. Of course, pulley-weight training is very specific, the swimming action in each style is closely copied with the swimmer either standing up or lying on an inclined bench. The bench (which is not absolutely necessary because the swimmer can stand) consists of a board about one foot wide at an angle of 30 degrees to the floor. The swimmer lies on the board face down, or on his back for backstroke. Pulley-weight training for all styles can be done in odd moments, on rising in the morning and before going to bed, and at times when crowded pools or unco-operative pool managers make water training impossible.

Girls and 'Bulk'

Males seem to be able to profit from a tremendous increase in muscularity of the upper body and swim very fast despite the increase in resistance in the water caused by the greater body mass. This is *plain fact* and a conclusion that we must draw from observation of present world record holders.

On the other hand, while it is important for girls to have well-developed, strong muscles in order to swim fast, recent observations we have made in Australia suggest that there is a point where increased bulk in the female results in worsened performance. If girls show obvious signs of over-development of muscles and of bulkiness, then I believe their strengthening training should be made distinctly less than for those girls who can retain slim, tapered bodies. I believe that girl swimmers benefit from a fair amount of strengthening work, particularly pulley-weight training and work with rubber bands (which we shall discuss later), but they probably do not require as much as boys for top performance. I feel certain that girls like Dawn Fraser and Lorraine Crapp would not have been such great champions *without* special strengthening exercises, but, I also believe that it is easily possible for some girls to do *too much* heavy work. Judgment of just how much weight-training girls should do is no easy matter and is a point at which coaching becomes an ART, because we have as yet no exact scientific rules to guide us.

The ideal to be aimed at for the girl swimmer is *strength with slimness and good streamlining*. Of course, how she will develop depends a lot on the heredity of the individual girl.

We cannot blame swimming or training in itself for making some girls 'too big.' Remember, there are vast numbers of girls who grow very large who have *never* trained for swimming or done any strengthening exercises. It is of great importance for girl swimmers in particular NOT TO OVER-EAT, especially foods rich in fats and carbohydrates.

All swimmers should try to eat natural foods and very little white bread, white flour and white-sugar products. They should concentrate on protein foods (lean meat and fish) and make a habit of cutting down on fatty foods. Boiled potatoes have about half the total fat of 'French fried' potatoes which must be avoided by the swimmer, especially if he or she is becoming too bulky. I believe that scientific control of food over a *long* period may play a very important part in developing the super athletes of the future, even though at present it might appear that some top sportsmen do eat 'anything' and get away with it. Girl swimmers must keep their bodies streamlined by moderate eating and by restricting their diet to natural foods (fruit, vegetables, eggs, lean meat and fish, etc.).

Exercise Programmes

Among our pupils, younger boys and girls carry out much the same general programme as older ones, except that they use lighter weights in the weight training.

In general we have selected those exercises which particularly strengthen the muscles of the upper body, and specifically the swimming muscles. Other exercises are included which increase flexibility of shoulder and ankle joints. You will notice that there are very few thigh-developing exercises like squatting carried out because we want swimmers with fairly slim tapered legs and thighs (like the great Swedish swimmer Arne Borg).

Static Weight Training (Isometric Contractions)

A relatively new method has been introduced into resistance exercises and is becoming very popular in many sporting circles. It is known as Isometric or Static contraction of muscles. An isometric contraction involves the muscle working against an immovable or nearly immovable resistance.

Supposing you take a bar-bell and 'press' it upwards from the chest so that the arms are fully extended above the head. In making ordinary repetitions, this is done with one main 'explosion' of energy so that the muscles of the shoulders, back and arms are strengthened mostly for *the first part* of this pressing movement. After this the weight 'flies' up to the final position with very little work done by the muscles in intermediate positions. When *isometric* contractions are made, a quite heavy weight is held for about 10 seconds or longer at various positions through the complete range of a movement. In this way the muscles are strengthened throughout their *whole* movement, not just in the initial contracting position.

Many weight trainers and some physical educators claim that static training of muscles is very much more effective in giving strength than the traditional isotonic weight training method. I am inclined to favour what has been called the *Intermediary Contraction* method. Here the contraction is made with heavy weights continuously but slowly, taking about 6 seconds to push the weight from the position of flexion to maximum extension of the muscle and 6 seconds returning to the starting position. During the off-season we make intermediary movements *after* the standard 3 × 10 repetitions in the Weight Training schedule. During the months of swimming competition, I recommend that the muscles be 'kept strong' with 5 or 10 minutes a day of selected Intermediary contraction exercises using just about the heaviest weights that the individual swimmer can manage.

Here are five different exercise schedules including a special schedule for weight training during the competitive season.

Schedule 1: Out-of-season weight training. (For Periods 1 and 2.)

Schedule 2: Exercises without weights for strengthening and flexibility. (Periods 1 and 2.)

Schedule 3: Pulley-weight strengthening for swimming. (Periods 1 to 4.)

Schedule 4: Weight training and other exercises for the competitive season and pre-race warm-up. (Periods 3 and 4.)

Schedule 5: Home Exercises. A half-hour schedule for swimmers. (Periods 1 and 2.)

Schedule 1
OUT-OF-SEASON WEIGHT TRAINING
(*For Periods* 1 *and* 2)

To the endurance and skill gained by swimming we must add muscular strength if a swimmer is to reach his best. We are of course training to strengthen the muscles for swimming and *not* to be champion weight-lifters. Instead of attempting nearly maximum lifts of 150 pounds or so like the weight-lifter, the swimmer (depending on age, sex and strength) will use weights from about 5 pounds (for eight-year-olds) to about 60 pounds.

You will notice that the tempo suggested for different exercises varies, being either slow, moderate or fast. The fast tempo should be at approximately the stroking rate of swimming. In this way you will help adapt the muscles for the swimming movements.

The number of repetitions and the weights used should gradually be increased from the first day of weight training. During the first weeks of training with weights, it is best to progress only slowly. A relatively light weight may be used for the first two weeks of weight training and then progress to a 'heavy' weight. We shall define here the 'heavy' weight as the weight with which the swimmer is only just able to make ten repetitions.

Here is a *rough* guide to the weights which may be used by various swimmers:

Boys over 16 years	40 to 60 pounds
Girls over 16	20 to 40 pounds
Boys 14 to 16	20 to 50 pounds
Girls 14 to 16	10 to 30 pounds
Boys and Girls 10 to 12	10 to 20 pounds
Boys and Girls 8 to 10	5 to 10 pounds

Progressive Table for Weight Training

Week by week the weight training should become harder.

Week 1: 10 repetitions of each exercise only.
            No more than three sessions per week.

Week 2: 2 × 10 repetitions.
            No more than three sessions per week.

Week 3: 2 × 10 repetitions, and also
            2 repetitions of Intermediary contractions for some exercises (see description above).
            Two or three sessions per week.

Week 4: The full programme –
and   3 × 10 repetitions, and also
after   10 repetitions of Intermediary contractions.
            Two or three sessions per week.

Stretching

When carrying out exercises with weights, even at fast tempo, it is very important to *stretch fully* the active muscles with each repetition. With the stretching there should be a momentary period of complete relaxation allowing the muscles to be 'pulled out' by the weight. In this way the *long* 'swimmer's muscles' will best be developed.

Making Your Bar-bells

A weight of up to 15 pounds or so can be provided by using plain bars of iron, but after the diameter becomes greater than about 1¼ inches the bars become too difficult to hold in the hands. To make heavier bar-bells, weights of some sort must be fixed on the ends of the bar. Iron weights are easiest to use but fairly expensive. However, it is possible to improvise by making bar-bells which have cement in jam tins at the ends. Coach Counsilman has improvised in this way for his squads. Of course, for the individual enthusiastic swimmer, if he can afford it, a shop-purchased bar-bell with adjustable weights is a good investment for life. After competitive swimming is finished, a little daily weight training can be important in maintaining fitness for everyday living.

Schedule 1

EXERCISES

1. *Warm-up Exercise.* (For 'warming-up' muscles throughout the body.)

Grasp bar-bell with the grip slightly wider than shoulder width. Place toes under bar with feet comfortably apart. With head up and legs slightly bent, pull the bar-bell to the chest. The pull from floor to chest is called a 'clean' in weight-lifting language.

Pause for a moment with the weight on the chest, and then with the legs straight and body erect push it to full arms' length overhead. The push overhead is called a 'press.'

Lower the weight to the chest and then to a position below the knees and *stretch downwards*. Repeat the clean and press, and downwards stretching movement.

After two or three weeks, work up to 3 × 10 repetitions at moderate tempo.

2. *Presses.* (Shoulder exercise, for strengthening the deltoids and the trapezius muscles.)

'Clean' the bar to the chest as in the warm-up exercise. With back straight press upwards, completely straightening arms with each movement. Lower the bar to the chest, repeat the press from the chest.

3 × 10 repetitions at fast tempo.

Then 10 repetitions slow movements. (Intermediary contractions.)

3. *Full Squats with Deep Breathing Without Weights.* (For agility and stamina.)

These squats of 'deep knee bends' are carried out at fast tempo, and only the body-weight is used. The main aims are to improve flexibility and increase the rate and depth of the breathing rather than to build up the mass of the leg muscles. Finely muscled, slender legs are better for swimmers than bulky muscular legs.

3 × 30 repetitions at moderate tempo.

As well as full respirations during the squats, each group of 30 repetitions should be followed by a deep breathing exercise to increase the flexibility of the rib cage. The arms are held out in front of the chest, palms touching. With each inspiration the arms are flung back as far as possible and brought together in front with each complete expiration.

Ten to fifteen deep breaths after each group of thirty squats.

4. *Pullovers.* (For the upper arm muscles and a breathing and chest expanding exercise.)

Lie on the back, if possible with a box or a bench under the chest, and hold the bar-bell with a wide grip and straight arms above the chest. Lower the bar-bell in a quarter circle arc until the arms are stretched back beyond the head, keeping the arms straight.

This exercise should be carried out at a slow tempo, inhaling completely while lowering the bar-bell and exhaling to a maximum while pulling back to the original position above the chest.

This pullover exercise is very valuable when carried out after each group of repetitions of squatting while recovering from the increased breathing.

Repeat 20 times at moderate tempo.

5. *Bent-forward Rowing.* (For strengthening muscles of the upper back and arms.)

Hold bar-bell with hands slightly wider than the shoulder width and lean forward at a right-angle. Keeping the back flat, pull the bar-bell to the body where the chest meets the upper abdomen. Then lower the barbell, allowing the momentarily relaxed arms to stretch down as completely as possible.

3 × 10 repetitions at fast tempo.

6. *Beginning-of-pull Strengthener.* (For strengthening the pectoral muscles on the front of the chest.)

Lie on the back holding bar with a close grip, arms stretched out behind the head, palms up. Lift the bar so that the straight arms make an angle of approximately 60 degrees to the floor. Then return to the starting position.

3 × 10 repetitions at moderate tempo.

7. *Bench Presses.* (For strengthening chest and shoulder muscles.)

Lie on the back (preferably over a box or bench) and hold the bar-bell across the chest with hands wider than the shoulder width. Push the weight directly over the chest, straightening the arms. Then lower the weight relaxing momentarily with the bar resting on the chest.

3 × 10 repetitions at fast tempo.

10 repetitions, slow movements. (Intermediary contractions.)

8. *Upright Rowing.* (For the shoulders and upper back, and strengthening both sections of the deltoids and the trapezius muscles.)

Hold the bar-bell with a narrow grip, palms towards the body, and raise it from a position across the thighs to the chin, keeping the elbows higher than the hands throughout and the back straight. Lower the bar, stretching the relaxed arm muscles fully.

3 × 10 repetitions at fast tempo.

Then 10 repetitions of slow movements. (Intermediary contractions.)

9. *Leg Raising.* (To strengthen the abdominal muscles.)

Lie on the back and grasp the bar-bell with straightened arms beyond the head. Lift the legs from the hips to make an angle of about 45 degrees with the floor. Point the toes.

3 × 10 repetitions at moderate tempo.

10. *Sit Forward Bending.* (To strengthen the lower back, increase hip and spinal flexibility and stretch the leg muscles.)

Sit with feet astride and hold the bar-bell behind the neck. Keep the legs straight and limber forward, attempting to place the forehead on the ground between the knees.

3 × 10 repetitions at moderate tempo.

11. *End-of-pull Strengthener.* (For the muscles involved in the end of the crawl-stroke arm pull. To strengthen the triceps of the upper arm and the deltoids of the shoulders.)

Stand with feet astride and bend forward with the trunk parallel to the ground. Hold the bar-bell resting on the buttocks with palms up. Push the weight as far out and up as possible, keeping the arms straight. Relax arm muscles and let the weight fall back to the buttocks.

3 × 10 repetitions at moderate tempo.

10 repetitions of slow movements. (Intermediary contractions.)

12. *Back of Head Push-ups.* (To strengthen deltoids and triceps. Stand with the bar behind the head and resting on the neck. With a narrow grip, press above head and straighten arms. Then lower the bar-bell *carefully* (or you will hit your head).

3 × 10 repetitions at fast tempo.

10 repetitions of slow movements. (Intermediary Contractions.)

13. *Forearm Rotation – The 'Counsilman Exercise.'* (An important exercise for strengthening the muscles involved in the rotating movement of the forearm which should be developed in all four swimming styles.)

Lie on the back. The bar-bell is held with the arms bent at right-angles at the elbows and flat on the floor. The upper arms remain on the floor throughout the exercise so that the points of the shoulders and elbows are all in a straight line. The bar is lifted with the forearm to the straight-up position, then lowered back to the floor.

3 × 10 repetitions moderate tempo.

10 repetitions of slow movements. (Intermediary contractions.)

14. *Downwards and Backwards Stretching.* (A finishing-off exercise to stretch the muscles generally.)

With feet astride, bend forward in a toe-touching fashion and grasp the bar with a wide grip. Limber down, keeping the legs and arms straight, at the same time relax as many muscles as possible. Then lift the weight to the chest and press it above the head. Stretch up and then stretch backwards as far as possible, still keeping balance. Return the bar-bell to the stretch-down position and limber downwards before repeating.

Repeat 20 times at slow tempo.

Remember in all exercises:
Stretch the muscles
as much as possible
with each repetition
This is important in developing the long
supple muscles which a swimmer needs.

Schedule 2

FLEXIBILITY AND STRENGTHENING EXERCISES WITHOUT WEIGHTS

This exercise programme, designed for swimmers, should be carried out for 15 or 20 minutes in conjunction with weight training, and should be used at open-air pools when cold water makes a *full* swimming programme impossible. First there are exercises for individuals and then 'doubles' exercises (for pairs of swimmers).

1. *Warm-up Exercises*

Running on-the-spot, lifting knees up high, with plenty of arm movement. Then jump up and down for 'skip-jumps' (the sort of jumps you do when skipping with a rope). Repeat for about 2 minutes.

2. *Shoulder Circling and Stretching*

Stand, with legs astride, then circle each arm separately, backwards then forwards. Then with both arms together, circle backwards and forwards. In each direction repeat 20 times.

Stand, with legs astride, finger-tips touching under the chin, elbows bent and at shoulder height. Keep the body straight and fling both arms back, stretching the shoulder joints so that the hands almost touch behind the shoulders, then return to the starting position. Repeat 20 times being careful not to bend the body forward.

3. *Backwards and Forwards Stretching*

Stand with legs astride, keeping knees straight, bend over and stretch down to put hands on the ground near the heels. Then swing hands up over the head, arms straight, and bend back as far as possible, dropping the head as far as you can to look behind you. Repeat 10 to 20 times fairly slowly, stretching as far as possible each time.

4. *Body Presses*

Lie face down with feet pointed, with weight of the body on the *tops* of your feet. Bend the arms and put your hands flat on the floor under your shoulders. Keeping the body very flat press up until your arms are straight, slowly bend your arms and lower the body until your nose just touches the ground – do not *lie down* on the ground, hold yourself straight supported on your hands and the tops of your feet. Young boys and girls and weaker swimmers will have to do body presses with the knees on the ground. Repeat slowly 10 to 20 times.

5. *Knees to Chin*

Lie flat on your back, hands behind your head. Keeping legs together, bring knees up to the chin, then stretch the legs out straight, keeping them just above the ground and the feet pointed. Repeat 10 to 20 times slowly. This is a good 'intermediary' exercise for the abdominal muscles.

6. *Pull Backs*

Lie face down, bend your knees, throw your head back and put your arms behind you to grasp your ankles with your hands. From this position pull back, trying to put your head on to your feet by lifting your chest and thighs off the ground – relax to put chest and thighs back on the ground, then pull back again. Repeat 10 to 20 times.

7. *Squat Thrusts. At a fast tempo*

Start from standing position. On the count of 'one' quickly bend knees to the full squat position, on count of 'two' throw the feet out behind you and put hands down flat on the ground under the shoulders so that you balance on the toes and hands, on count of 'three' jump the feet back to the hands but keep the knees well bent, and on count of 'four' resume the initial standing position again. Repeat at fast tempo for as many times as possible, 10 to 20 repetitions.

8. *Leg Lifting*
Lie flat on the back, arms stretched out behind the head. Keeping the legs straight and feet pointed, lift the legs up, but to not more than 45 degrees above the ground. Slowly lower the legs but do not let the feet touch the ground. Hold the legs out for five seconds with heels one inch above the ground. Repeat slowly 10 to 20 times.

9. *Arm Flutters*
Lie face down with arms stretched beyond your head and feet pointed. Lift your chest and arms up off the ground. Keeping the arms straight lift them alternately up and down but do not let the hands or arms touch the ground. Repeat 10 to 20 times at fast tempo.

10. *Sit-ups*
Lie flat on the back, hands behind the head. Keeping the legs on the ground, swing up to put the head down on the knees, then slowly lie down again. Keep the feet pointed. Repeat 10 to 20 times.

11. *Ankle Stretching*
Kneeling with heels close together and feet pointed, sit back on the heels, then swing slowly back to stretch the ankle joints using the hands for support on the floor. Repeat 10 to 20 times, slowly.

12. *Ankle Joint Flexibility*
Stand up (holding a support if possible) and lift one foot off the ground. Stretch the foot and shake it vigorously making the ankle joint as loose as possible. Repeat with other foot. Thirty seconds shaking for each foot.

Doubles Exercises (*Exercises in pairs*)
Do these exercises with a partner about your own weight.

1. *Bend-Backs*
The two swimmers kneel down facing each other with their knees just touching. Swimmer A puts his hands on the top of the thighs of swimmer B and pushes down hard. With his hands resting across the chest, swimmer B bends back until his head touches the ground and then straightens up and pushes down on

the thighs of swimmer A, who bends back. Repeat, for 10 to 20 bend-backs each.

2. *Chest Raising*

Swimmer A lies face down with hands clasped behind his neck and feet pointed with swimmer B holding his ankles down. Swimmer A lifts his chest high up off the ground and bends back as far as he can. He then comes down to a position with his chest just off the ground (about one inch). Do not allow the chest to touch the ground during this exercise. Repeat 10 to 20 times for each swimmer.

3. *Sideways Twisting*

A and B assume the same positions as for the previous exercise but A has his legs about 12 inches apart. Then A, keeping his chest an inch or so above the ground, swings his upper body around sideways as far as he can towards his hip and then as far as he can towards the other hip. Repeat 10 to 20 times for each swimmer.

4. *Doubles Push-ups*

Swimmer A lies down flat on his back with his elbows on the ground beyond his head in the 'folded arm position' (with right hand holding left elbow, left hand holding right elbow). B stands with one foot on either side of A with feet as near A's ankles as possible and leans forward with his legs and body straight to put his hands on A's elbows. From this position, swimmer A pushes upwards and forwards with his arms against the body weight of swimmer B. A pushes up until his arms are above his chest, then he slowly lowers his arms back to the floor. Swimmer B keeps a continuous pressure against the elbows of A both during the arm lift and also as A lowers his arms back. Repeat 10 to 20 times each swimmer.

5. *Partner Lifting*

Stand back to back with arms linked (A's right arm linked through B's left arm, etc.). Then A bends forward to lift B off the ground taking B's weight on his back, then A returns B slowly to the standing position. Repeat, alternately 10 to 20 times for each swimmer.

6. *Doubles Shoulder Pressing*

Stand facing each other, both bend forward and put your

hands on each other's shoulders. Both swimmers push downwards hard to make isometric contractions and strengthen the arm and shoulder muscles. Repeat for half minute to one minute.

7. *Ankle Twisting*

In pairs, swimmer A sits and B kneels down and grasps A's foot in his hands. B twists A's foot in all directions, A makes the muscles around the ankle joint as loose and relaxed as possible. Then B changes to A's other foot and does the same. Change over so that A twists B's feet.

Schedule 3
PULLEY WEIGHTS

Using the pulley-weight machine is a good way of strengthening the muscles which are particularly needed in the four styles of swimming. Pulley-weight work should be done in addition to weight training and other exercises which help to make the swimmer strong and flexible. It is probably best to use the machine while lying on the 30 degrees inclined bench, but it is not essential. The swimmer may do the exercises standing up.

A 'half-reducing' pulley system is recommended so that the weights travel half the vertical distance moved by the hands. This enables the best use of the apparatus and the pulleys absorb most of the sudden dragging effect of the weights which would occur in a simple single pulley system as the arms come forward.

Bob Kiphuth at Yale, who used pulley-weights for strengthening swimmers in the 1930s, well describes their use in his book *Swimming* (Barnes and Co., New York, 1942).

It is not easy to say exactly what weights are necessary for various individuals, but as a rough guide I would say that the total load on each side of the machine should be between ten pounds and twenty pounds, depending on the strength of the swimmer.

The Use of Machine

During the non-competitive season (Periods 1 and 2), strength and endurance may be built up with 15 minutes to 30 minutes per day (divided into two or more sessions).

During the competitive season from 5 minutes to 15 minutes a day may be spent with the apparatus depending on the amount of water training which can be done at the time. Lack of water training can to some extent be made up by work with the pulley-weights.

Method of Use

The swimmer should experiment by changing his position relative to the pulley-weight machine to enable all parts of the pull (beginning, middle, and end) to be strengthened in various strokes.

The exercises should be carried out in 1, 2 and 5 minute bursts with 1 minute rests. This is of course an *interval* training method. Weights should be relatively heavy for each individual so that working at fast (swimming) tempo he can only just complete the full time set for each exercise.

For the first two weeks, relatively light weights should be used as the swimmer adapts himself, but as training on the machine progresses, gradually heavier weights should be used. It is not much use if the weights are too light for the individual. The swimmer should spend about half his time training at his 'major' style and half his time at the other styles. The pulley-weight machine is a wonderful strengthener and should be used by all serious competitive swimmers. Details of the weight training (time, weights used, etc.) should of course be written up daily with other particulars of training in the swimmer's personal log book which, incidentally, should be kept written up for every day of the year – even when you do 'nothing.'

Rubbers

Recently we have been experimenting with the use of half-inch diameter rubber for pulley-weight type of exercises and isometric work in the various positions of the arm pull.

It is possible with half-inch-diameter rubbers to obtain a very much stronger resistance than with pulley-weights. About ten feet of good quality spear-gun rubber can be obtained at a fraction of the cost of a pulley-weight machine.

I am inclined to think that in the future we may largely replace the cumbersome and more expensive pulley-weight machine with the simple rubbers, which can be easily set up in any place, even a bedroom. An inclined bench can still be used.

The Victory ceremony, Leipzig, August 1962. Adri Lasterie (Holland) in the centre has won the 400 metres individual medley race in European Record time of 5 minutes 27.8 seconds. On the left is Britain's great Anita Lonsborough (Olympic, European and Empire breaststroke champion) who was second. The third girl is M. Egervari (Hungary) who made a National record in the race.

John Konrads and Dawn Fraser, two Australian swimmers whose performances shook the swimming world during the Australian 'revival.' Between 1958 and 1961 John Konrads broke every world freestyle record from 200 metres to 1,650 yards. Perhaps his greatest swim was his world record performance for 1,650 yards (and 1,500 metres) of 17 minutes 11 seconds made at the North Sydney Olympic pool on February 27, 1960. Dawn Fraser in November 1962 at the age of 24 did the 'impossible' when she broke the minute with 59.5 seconds for 110 yards and 100 metres. The performance established her as the greatest female swimmer the world has seen. Then on February 29, 1964, Dawn further reduced her World Record to 58.9 seconds.

Schedule 4
FOR THE COMPETITIVE SEASON AND FOR PRE-RACE
WARM-UP

I believe that about ten minutes per day should be spent on weight training, rubbers and other exercises when very hard swimming training is being carried out, and up to thirty minutes when only half to one hour per day is used for swimming.

Each swimmer should have a schedule of exercises suitable for the conditions prevailing. Swimmers should know the following summer exercise schedule well, so that they can go ahead and start exercising before swimming or at home, whether the coach is present or not. Naturally it is best if weights can be kept and used at the pool.

It is important to keep the muscles strong with some weight-training all through the competitive season. Many world record-holders nowadays train with weights right up to the day of important races. I have used some weight training exercises even as part of the pre-race warm-up with my swimmers and we often take bar-bells or rubbers to the competition pool for this purpose. Before a competition on a cold day in open pools I believe it is sometimes better to warm up with weights rather than go into the water, particularly if no hot shower is available.

Here is a specimen programme of exercises which may be used as a short schedule before training sessions, and for pre-race warming-up. If, however, there is only limited time available for swimming, then it is obviously not a good idea to spend time doing exercises, leaving the pool empty with nobody swimming.

Often bar-bells will not be available at the pool, then only the free standing exercises can be done.

WITH WEIGHTS. 10 to 60 pounds (heavy enough just to allow 10 repetitions at slow tempo).

1. *Warm-up Exercise*
   See Exercise 1 in Schedule 1. Repeat 10 to 20 times.

2. *Bent-forward Rowing*
   See Exercise 5 in Schedule 1. Repeat 10 to 20 times.

3. *Forearm Rotations* (in standing position)
   Stand with the feet comfortably astride. With hands at

c

shoulder width apart and palms facing upwards hold the bar-bell behind the head with the elbows out to the side at shoulder height. Then moving only the forearms and wrists bring the bar-bell forward in a quarter circle until it is straight above your head. Relax your forearms and wrists to lower the bar-bell back to the starting position. Repeat 10 to 20 times at slow tempo.

4. *End-of-pull Strengthener*
See Exercise 11 in Schedule 1. 10 repetitions of slow movements.

5. *Back-of-head Push-ups*
See Exercise 12 in Schedule 1. 10 repetitions of slow movements.

EXERCISES WITHOUT WEIGHTS

6. *Shoulder Circling and Stretching*
See Exercise 2 in Schedule 2. Repeat for 1 minute.

7. *Body Presses*
See Exercise 4 in Schedule 2. Repeat 10 to 20 times.

8. *Pull-backs*
See Exercise 6 in Schedule 2. Repeat 10 to 20 times.

9. *Sit-ups*
See Exercise 10 in Schedule 2. Repeat 10 to 20 times.

10. *Squats*
Stand with the feet a little apart and keep the heels on the ground during the knee bends (or squats). Position of hands optional. Do 10 to 20 squats.

11. *Leg Lifting*
See Exercise 8 in Schedule 2. Repeat slowly 10 to 20 times.

12. *Ankle Stretching*
See Exercise 11 in Schedule 2. Repeat 10 to 20 times slowly.

13. *Dive Loosening*
Stand with the feet a little apart in a starting dive position, knees slightly bent and arms hanging loosely at your sides. Bend forward until your hands almost touch the ground, drop the head forward by relaxing the neck muscles. Then swing both arms backwards and forwards, moderately bending and

straightening the knees every time the arms pass them. Muscles should be as relaxed as possible and the movements should be smooth and flowing. This is a good general loosener for swimming. Repeat 10 to 20 times.

Schedule 5
HALF-HOUR HOME EXERCISE SCHEDULE
For strength and flexibility of swimmers of all ages. To be carried out from time to time at home, *in addition to* weight training, work with pulley-weights or rubbers, and group exercises.

1. *Dive Loosening – Standing*   *Repeat for 2 minutes*
See Exercise 13 in Schedule 4.

2. *Leg Kicking – Lying Face Down on Floor*   *For 2 minutes*
With legs straight and *feet pointed,* crawl kick at a fast rate keeping the legs straight. Rest for five seconds every half minute, or when fatigue makes it absolutely necessary.

3. *Beginning-of-pull Strengthener – Lying on Back*
For 2 minutes
Lie on back, arms stretched beyond head, hold hand-weights with palms up. Lift the weights *alternately* about one foot from ground and lower. The exercise is to be carried out at a fairly fast tempo. Rest for five seconds every half minute, or when absolutely necessary.

Note on Handweights: Boys over 13 years use 6 inches of $1\frac{1}{2}$-inch-diameter steel bar. Dumb-bells may of course be used for this exercise, between two and eight pounds depending on the strength of the swimmer.

4. *Sit-up Bend Forward – Lying on Back*   *For 2 minutes*
Lying on back, legs spread, arms extended beyond head. In a swinging movement sit up, place hands behind the neck and bend the back as much as possible pushing the head on to the ground. Point the toes. Repeat 2 minutes.

5. *Swing-up, Swing-down – Standing with Feet Astride*
For 2 minutes
Standing with legs astride, hold a hand-weight above the head in both hands, swing the body down to push the head between

the legs and up again in a flowing, easy movement. Stretch up and stretch down, keeping the knees pressed back.

6. *Body Presses – Body Press Position*   *For 2 minutes*
See Exercise 4 in Schedule 2.

7. *Pull-backs – Lying Face Down*   *For 2 minutes*
See Exercise 6 in Schedule 2.

8. *Beginning of Pull Strengthener – Lying on Back*
     For 2 minutes
Two more minutes of this important exercise as described in Exercise 3 of this schedule.

9. *Squat-Thrusts – Standing*   *For 2 minutes*
See Exercise 7 in Schedule 2.

10. *Deep Breathing After Squat-Thrusts Exercise – Standing*
     For 1 minute
Breathe in through mouth and out through mouth and nose (as in swimming). Fling arms backwards during inspiration.

11. *Beginning-of-pull Strengthener – Lying on Back*
     For 1 minute
Third repetition of this important exercise described in Exercise 3 of this schedule.

12. *Shoulder Flexibility – Standing*   *For 2 minutes*
Grasping a towel or stick with the hands as close together as possible and arms straight, circle the arms backwards and forwards overhead. Repeat this flexibility exercise for 2 minutes. After a week or so of practice the hands can gradually be brought closer together.

13. *Shoulder Loosening, with Hand-weights – Standing Astride*
     For 1 minute
Bend slightly forward and hold the hand-weights. Whilst keeping the trunk firm and the head still, circle each shoulder alternately in the loosest possible manner. Swing each arm first clockwise and then in anti-clockwise direction.

14. *Ankle Circling – Sitting*   *For 2 minutes*
Sit on ground or in a chair. With legs straight and heels off the ground, circle and twist the ankles in all directions. An

assistant (or parent) can help here to stretch the ankles. Flexible joints are very important in all swimming styles.

15. *Ankle Stretch Pointing – Kneel on Floor*   *For 2 minutes*
   Kneel and sit on the ankles with the heels close together and toes well pointed. Use the weight of the body to force the foot gradually into a more pointed position. Concentrate on stretching one ankle-joint at a time.

16. *Leg Loosening – Standing with Support*   *For 1 minute*
   Stand on one leg and then the other and shake the free leg vigorously from the hip down, aiming at the loose, flipping action of the ankles necessary for all styles.

17. *Dive Loosening – Standing*   *For 1 minute*
   Repeat as in Exercise 1.   *Total exercising time:* 31 *minutes*

NOTE: A minute clock should be clearly visible. If the times suggested are followed, it will take just 31 minutes to complete the schedule. For a 15 minute exercise period the times suggested for each exercise may be halved.
REMEMBER: During Periods 1 and 2 we encourage our pupils to exercise morning and night five or six days a week. Even five minutes is better than nothing. The exercises may include either:

1. The Home Exercise Schedule $\frac{1}{4}$ to $\frac{1}{2}$ hour/day
   and/or
2. Pulley-weights $\frac{1}{4}$ to $\frac{1}{2}$ hour/day
   and/or
3. Weight-training Schedule $\frac{1}{4}$ to $\frac{1}{2}$ hour/day
   and/or
4. Work with Rubbers $\frac{1}{4}$ to $\frac{1}{2}$ hour/day

It is important for the swimmer to make a regular *habit* of doing *some* flexibility and strengthening exercises, but you will notice that I have not categorically set down that the swimmer *must* do so many hours a day. This is because individuals will vary in the amounts of strengthening and body-building work they need, and in the amounts of other exercise and conditioning work (such as football, hockey, cross-country running, etc.) that they may be doing.

I believe that strengthening exercises play an important part *early* in a swimmer's career but that less need be done once he has become strong and has built up the necessary muscles. I believe that in future isometric work using the resistance of strong rubbers, concentrating on strengthening the specific muscles involved in the various parts of the stroke, will prove to be of great value to swimmers.

It could prove best for girls who fear they 'will become too big to fit into their wedding dresses' to concentrate on training the specific swimming muscles with isometric work, using rubbers and not doing much work with weights once they have built up reasonable upper-body strength.

The schedules set out here should serve as a guide. I believe that exercises are important, but that swimmers, particularly older ones, must often be treated as individuals requiring differing programmes.

CHAPTER SIX

Food for Swimmers

To perform at one's best, in swimming – in fact in everyday life – it is essential to make a habit of eating the most nutritious foods, and to follow this all through your life.

The very best diet consists of a WIDE VARIETY OF FOODS AS NEAR AS POSSIBLE TO THEIR NATURAL STATE.

Hans Selye has shown that guinea-pigs on a protein-rich diet can best withstand stress. There are strong indications that the best diet for physical vigour and good health consists of a large proportion of protein foods and fruit and vegetables, but including only relatively small amounts of the concentrated carbohydrate foods (except in the special case of the *pre-race* meal – see pages 35 and 73).

The *chief protein foods* are meat, fish, poultry, eggs, cheese and milk.

The *concentrated carbohydrate foods to be avoided* in the everyday diet include sugar and sugar products, jam, chocolates and confectionery, white bread, cakes, biscuits, pastry and all soft drinks. Ice-cream, because it contains a large percentage of sugar and fat, should be regarded as an occasional luxury.

As soon as primitive peoples, such as the Australian aborigines learn to eat a 'civilised' diet of white bread, tea, sugar and jam (mainly carbohydrates), they lose their natural vigour and their health deteriorates.

A Guide to Good Eating

EAT SPARINGLY	EAT THESE FOODS
White sugar and jam.	Honey, marmite, peanut butter.
White and ordinary 'brown' bread.	Whole grain bread, rye bread and crushed wheat bread.

EAT SPARINGLY	EAT THESE FOODS
Cakes, biscuits and pastry. Always avoid foods made mainly with white flour and sugar.	Using whole grain flour, wheat germ and dried fruits, very nutritious cakes and cookies can be made.
Chocolates and confectionery.	Sultanas and raisins, all dried fruits, peanuts, almonds and nuts.
All soft drinks and artificial flavourings which are fairly concentrated solutions of sugar.	Milk and pure fruit juices, or fresh fruit, e.g. oranges.
Spaghetti and macaroni.	Meat, fish, poultry, eggs, cheese. Liver and kidney are excellent meats and should if possible be eaten often.
Prepared rice and cornflake-type breakfast cereals; particularly avoiding sugar-frosted and chocolate coated types.	Whole grain porridge if possible, or use packaged cereals prepared from *whole* wheat. Add one or two dessertspoons of wheat germ, and honey for sweetening.

Remember, all meals should contain plenty of protein foods and either fruit or vegetables – cutting down on the carbohydrate foods mentioned in the left-hand column above.

EXTRA VITAMINS

Individuals engaged in strenuous physical activity use more of certain vitamins than does the average person, so it is reasonable that besides eating natural foods, extra vitamins should be taken by those training for sport. These vitamins should include:

The B-Complex group.

Vitamin C.

Vitamin E and possibly Wheat Germ Oil which may contain endurance promoting factors in addition to the Vitamin E (alpha tocopheral).

Many sportsmen also need to take some form of IRON to help

Coach Jim Counsilman in his pool-side gym at the Indiana University. Here
he supervises two of his squad in static, Isometric Contraction exercises aimed
at the development of the muscles specifically used in swimming. On the top
right is the large minute clock, an essential aid in modern swimming training.
During the last ten years or so thousands of these minute clocks have been
installed in pools all over the world. One of the original clocks (1946) can be seen
today at the North Sydney Olympic Pool.

Exercising on a warm day before starting the training session in the water. Generally our Ryde swimmers wear their track suits to do their weight work and flexibility exercises. We keep a wide variety of weights, from 5 lb. to 60 lb. in our coaches' room at the poolside.

make the red cells of the blood. Because it inactivates Vitamin E, iron should not taken within four hours of taking Vitamin E.

Here are some examples of meal menus, making use of the best foods.

BREAKFAST. Milk or pure fruit juice to drink. Wholemeal porridge, mixed grain or millet porridge, packaged wheat cereal, or 'Breakfast Brew' (see recipe). To any of the above add wheat germ, and use honey or sultanas to sweeten.

Highly Nutritious 'Breakfast Brew'
This may be eaten instead of a cold breakfast cereal. It may be cooked at home (possibly the night before) and placed in a wide-mouthed vacuum flask. The 'brew' may then be eaten in the morning before going to training or kept for a hot breakfast at the pool after training before going straight to school. This breakfast brew, being semi-liquid and easily digested, makes a good pre-race meal, especially when the porridge is finely ground.

Using a whole grain porridge or millet meal as a base, mix in:
Wheat germ (about one tablespoon).
Sultanas or raisins.
Powdered milk.
Honey if desired – or it can be added later.
Simmer for about ¼ hour.

Also suitable for breakfast are: Eggs – poached, boiled, scrambled, etc. Fish – grilled, poached, steamed, etc., or tinned fish, herrings, kippers, etc. Meat – lean grilled chops, steak, liver, kidneys, brains, etc. Cottage cheese is 'non-fattening' and an excellent protein food.

A GOOD PACKAGED LUNCH can be provided without using white bread sandwiches – use instead a whole-grain bread, and pack a salad in a plastic box or bag and include cheese, hard-boiled eggs, cold meat, a small tin of tongue or fish, and fresh fruit with some dried fruit, e.g. sultanas or raisins, to finish off.

DINNER. Concentrate on the protein foods – all types of meat, fish (fresh, tinned or frozen), poultry, etc., and plenty of vegetables. Follow the main course with fresh fruit, non-carbohydrate desserts like baked apples, baked custard and stewed fruits, or serve dried fruits and nuts and cheese.

Drink milk or pure fruit juices. If you are worried about putting on too much weight then drink skimmed (cream-free) milk.

FOR BETWEEN-MEAL SNACKS, eat fruits, or sultanas, raisins and nuts or whole grain bread and honey.

EATING 'OUT'! You do not have to appear a 'crank' to make a habit of eating nutritionally good foods. When you eat 'out' it is nearly always possible to choose the right things without making a fuss and embarrassing your friends, who may not be so particular about food. In any case you need not be *too* rigid, it is always possible to have the occasional 'luxury.' It is a pity that most kiosks sell mainly sweets and soft drinks – but even there you can usually choose milk and peanuts (the natural foods).

Fatty Foods. Everybody needs *some* fat in the diet, but grilled or steamed food is much more easily digested than fried food, which should be eaten sparingly by anyone, particularly the swimmer in training. Just before a race, the best food is one that is easily digested and does not lie in the stomach for a long time as fatty foods do.

Liver. (Lamb's or Calf's). This is a wonderful food, and should, if possible, be eaten about twice a week, and more often if your blood haemoglobin concentration is known to be low (that is, if you are anaemic).

Natural Foods. Although it is important that natural foods should be the key-note of the diet, at the same time common sense should be used. If a natural food – it could be wheat germ or raw carrot – disagrees with you, or if you dislike it strongly, then it can be avoided. Many foods *must* be cooked to make them edible – for instance, it would be stupid to try eating *raw* potato or raw whole wheat – this would be carrying the natural foods idea too far. Incidentally, potatoes are quite a good food (unless you need to lose weight) particularly if they are cooked in their skins.

Finally remember to aim at all times, now, and even when you stop training for swimming, at eating a wide variety of foods as near as possible to their natural state. This may be said to be the modern Gospel of good nutrition.

PART II
SCIENCE AND
SWIMMING PERFORMANCE

CHAPTER SEVEN

Swimmers and Vitamin Pills

WHEN we started coaching in Holland in 1962 I had two major disagreements with the Medical Committee of the Royal Dutch Swimming Association. One was on the question of whether there should be almost unrestricted training and racing of young swimmers, as in Australia and the U.S.A. (of course I argued 'swim them'). The other argument was on the question of whether swimmers in hard training were likely to benefit by supplementing their normal diets with various vitamin preparations.

Although it was generally agreed that taking extra vitamins could scarcely be called 'doping,' the Dutch Medical Committee nevertheless came down strongly *against* the practice. They held that it was unproven that extra vitamins were of any possible use with an 'adequate diet,' and were therefore at best a waste of money.

Our 'battle' on vitamins is still waging.

In almost every country it is common practice nowadays for coaches to supplement the diets of swimmers with additional vitamins, usually in quantities far in excess of the recommended minimum required for the health of a normal person.

It has been said by those who argue against extra vitamins that the sewers of some cities would provide the world's richest source of vitamins, so much of the millions of vitamin pills pass through the body unchanged and are wastefully excreted.

Mainly on the grounds of waste and expense, swimming coaches in general and at times myself in particular have been criticised by physicians and some academic people as being at the best misguided, and at worst charlatans. A professor of pharmacology at an Australian University has criticised my advocating vitamin supplementation for swimmers. Although it did not refer specifically to the needs of sportsmen, a leading article in the *Medical Journal of Australia* (September 23, 1961) pointed out that the danger of *poisoning* with very large doses of Vitamin A and D, and implied that in view of this, general vitamin supplementation was to be avoided. It was ironical that the same journal a month earlier (on August 19, 1961) had published an excellent scientific study proving that in a large group of ordinary men and women the incidence of coronary heart disease was significantly lower (5.8% as compared with 15.8% in an untreated control group) when *otherwise normal diets* were supplemented with moderate doses of vitamins A and D.

In the scientific literature there are studies which conclude that the average person on a normal diet does *not* benefit by general vitamin supplementation. On the other hand, to refute this *negative* evidence, which was based on the fact that changes could not be detected, there is a large volume of evidence showing that supplementation with various vitamins *is* beneficial, particularly where hard and prolonged muscular exercise is being carried out. Admittedly some of the experiments offered as 'proof' of the benefits of supplementation were not adequately controlled and did not allow for possible psychological effects, and on this account cannot be accepted without reservation.

Perhaps the reason for some of the negative results obtained is that often the study has been made on subjects carrying out only *average* activity and possibly already on an adequate diet. Often poor experimentation or insufficient observations can result in the answer 'unproved.' Where there is proper control of experiments, even a few *positive* conclusions in favour of supplementation mean more than a number of negative findings.

Not a great deal of research work has been carried out with active sportsmen in *severe* training, but where it has, the conclusions in the main support the principle of giving extra vitamins, and show that the body stressed by hard training is capable of improved performance after various vitamins have been added to the diet.

We are not discussing *drugs* but *vitamins*, accessory substances present in food; there can therefore be no objection on moral grounds to taking concentrated vitamins, any more than there could be to eating a teaspoonful of glucose before a race. The question to be answered satisfactorily is 'do extra vitamins help physical performance?'

Theoretically it would seem logical to expect that sportsmen carrying out the exercise required in hard training would need more vitamins, because it is known for certain that various vitamins play an important part in the chemistry of muscular metabolism.

VITAMINS A AND D

With a varied diet including reasonable amounts of dairy products and yellow vegetables, it is difficult for a person to avoid having more than adequate amounts of these fat-soluble vitamins, and there is little evidence that supplementation improves physical performance. As has been mentioned above, these two vitamins can, when taken in excess, be toxic. However, to have an adverse effect on the body it would appear[1] (see list of references at end of chapter) that very large quantities of both A and D would have to be taken – at least ten times the normal therapeutic dose, and this over long periods.

VITAMIN B COMPLEX

There appears to be a good deal of evidence that taking extra vitamin B complex, vitamin C and vitamin E (alpha tocopherol) can improve performance.

There are twelve known nutritive factors present in the vitamin B complex but only six of these are believed to be involved in deficiency diseases, the most common dietary shortages being of thiamin (B1) and riboflavin (B2).

Usually a number of members of the B complex group are administered together on the theory that a multiple deficiency often occurs.

Bicknell and Prescott[2] have stated that the thiamin requirement of an individual may be increased by *fifteen times* in severe exercise which means that the recognised daily requirement, 1.5 mg. per day for a sedentary man would, in severe exercise, be increased to about 22.5 mg. Bourne[3] has calculated that for this quantity of vitamin B1 to be ingested all of the following rich sources of the B complex would need to be consumed: 3 lb of wheatmeal bread, 2 lb of commercial wheat germ, ¼ lb of dried brewers' yeast and 5 lb of lean meat – clearly beyond the capacity of the human stomach, even of the hungriest of swimmers!

As Bourne points out, if the requirement of B1 is so greatly increased in severe muscular exercise it is highly probable that other members of the vitamin B complex, such as riboflavin and nicotinic acid, may be required in similarly increased amounts. Bourne reports that in his experiments rats injected with B complex ran longer on a treadmill before becoming fatigued than did untreated rats, whilst Gounelle[4] with cyclists and McCormick[5] with swimmers concluded from their experiments that supplementation of diets with B1 improved performance. Experiments with humans may at times be criticised on the score of psychological effects, but it could hardly be claimed that the rats performed better because they had faith in vitamin B1 or in the injections!

Doroschuk and Cureton[6] in a recent article state, 'There is no doubt that hard work demands not only increased calorie intake but also an increase in vitamins.' They cite two Russian research workers, Lauschner[7] and Yakavlew as reporting deficiencies created by hard physical work in people in construction gangs, even after supplementation. It was concluded by the Russian scientists that up to six times the U.S.A. daily recommended dose of vitamin B1 should be fed to athletes in training.

VITAMIN C (ASCORBIC ACID)

On theoretical grounds there appears to be good argument for everyone taking more than the minimum daily dose of vitamin C (25 mg. of ascorbic acid) which is recognised as essential to prevent signs of scurvy.

There is a high concentration of ascorbic acid in the cortex of the adrenal glands. Selye[8] drew attention to the fact that the adrenal cortex was involved in the response of the body to a number of stresses, including muscular exercise. Then Sayers[9] demonstrated that response to conditions of stress is accompanied by depletion of ascorbic acid in the adrenal cortex gland.

Dugal and Therian[10] found that in rats large doses protected them from the stress of cold as measured by the survival rate, and prevented hypertrophy of the adrenals.

Baccus and Toompas[11] showed that after pretreatment with the vitamin, rats exposed to a variety of stresses showed a decrease in many signs of Selye's alarm reaction.

Harris[12] has shown that common infections lower urinary

output of ascorbic acid in man whilst Bantwell[13] published evidence of increased use of vitamin C in the body under conditions of oxygen deficiency (a state of affairs constantly induced in training). Pirani[14] summed the matter up in 1952 by saying, 'It is generally agreed that tissue requirements for ascorbic acid are increased under conditions of increased body metabolism, and any stress if sufficiently severe and prolonged will cause a diminution of ascorbic acid concentration in the tissues, and as a rule more severely in the adrenals.'

Because there seemed ample grounds for the hypothesis that the young swimmer in hard training may easily deplete his ascorbic acid stores while on the ordinary schoolboy diet, the writer[15] carried out a series of experiments in 1951 with a group of swimmers including two who later became Olympians, Jon Henricks and David Hawkins. The following conclusions were reached. Before supplementation, although their diets *appeared* to contain even above average amounts of vitamin C, there was evidence from urinary excretion studies of a level of stored ascorbic acid so low as to be close to that reported for scurvy patients.

Then the subjects were given large doses of ascorbic acid. From the amount recovered in their urine after the tissues were saturated, it appeared that an average of 100 mg. per day was being utilised in the body, even when the training was not particularly severe. That amount (100 mg.) was well above the 30 to 75 mg. per day recommended by the British Medical Research Council and American National Research Council.

The point is, of course, that medically recommended intakes are for *normal* individuals, not swimmers covering up to seven miles training a day.

Ascorbic acid is relatively cheap and non-toxic. Beckman[1] reports that huge doses have been taken experimentally without harm, even up to 10 grams daily (more than 200 times the recommended dose). After the tissues are saturated, excess is excreted from the body.

Cureton[6] reports the Pole, Namyslowski, as showing that strenuous exercise produced a state of vitamin C deficiency and that he recommends 200 to 250 mg. daily at ski-ing camps.

Cureton reports that vitamin C supplementation is carried out during the competitive season by all U.S.S.R. athletes and most of all by long-distance runners. The majority of Australia's top swimmers in recent years have supplemented their diets, during hard training, with between 100 to 300 mg. of vitamin C per day.

VITAMIN E

This consists of a number of related substances, alpha, beta, gamma and delta tocopherols, found mainly in the tissues of plants and in high concentration in the embryo (the germ) of wheat. The *alpha* tocopherol has been found to have by far the greatest biological activity.

The naturally occurring a-alpha tocopherol acetate has a biological strength 36% greater than an equal weight of the synthetic form of the vitamin. However, the synthetic form is cheaper.

Even by 1955 when an International Conference on vitamin E was held in Venice there had been at least 4,000 publications on the vitamin. By 1963 there were probably 10,000 or more scientific papers published on vitamin E. There has been a tremendous controversy in medical circles about its effectiveness in a number of conditions including heart and circulatory diseases, skin diseases and muscular dystrophy. It has been argued recently that the reason for negative results has often been because doses of far too low a potency have been used. It is now generally agreed that at least 400 to 600 mg. per day is necessary to help many conditions. The Canadian physician Evan Shute,[16] who has argued strongly for wider use of alpha tocopherol, has said: 'All sorts of patients receiving no obvious help from 300 to 400 mg. have been helped remarkably by 600 to 2,400 as a daily dose. If there is a dam which prevents alpha tocopherol from getting into the circulation and tissues we propose to raise the tocopherol level until it *runs over the dam.* Half a dose of alpha tocopherol does *not* do half a job. . . . Let us emphasise this point. If you use vitamin E use enough.'

The first observed function of vitamin E on deprived rats was an anti-sterility effect, hence its popular but inaccurate name of the 'sex vitamin.' There has been no scientific evidence of alpha tocopherol producing abnormal sexual function in individuals receiving even very large doses. Vitamin E, in fact, has a general but as yet not completely understood function in metabolism,

and seems to have a particular effect on the physiology of muscle
(including heart muscle).

In the volume 'Vitamin E' (the 631-page record of proceedings
of the 1955 Congress) it is stated in summary, 'An important
effect of vitamin E is combating certain stress situations,
whether the stress factor is one of environment or of any combination of circumstances which PLACES A STRAIN ON THE
ORGANISM. Stress probably increases the tocopherol requirement of the organism.'

This would indicate the rationality of supplementing the diets
of sportsmen in hard training with vitamin E.

In all work with procedures or foods to improve performance,
because of the strong possibility of the psychological effect of
suggestion, the most convincing experiments are those which are
scientifically controlled. One method of control is to give half
the subjects the actual vitamin and the other half, unknowingly,
an inactive placebo dose. Control can be improved further by
the use of a 'double blind' experimental method where neither
subject *nor experimenter* knows what has been taken until all
results are collected and analysed. Experiments with animals,
particularly the guinea-pig and rat whose physiologies are quite
similar to man's, can also provide very useful evidence.

There are many very convincing experiments indicating that
athletic performance has been improved by supplementation
with alpha tocopherol. Much of this evidence has been brought
forward by Professor Cureton who has championed the use of
wheat germ and wheat germ oil. Cureton has told me that he
does not believe that alpha tocopherol is the most important
substance in wheat germ oil affecting endurance, but that it is a
different substance, a chemical whose structural formula has
now been worked out.

In a paper presented at the Conference of the Australian
Sports Medicine Association in Melbourne, 1956, Cureton recalled that the first experiments on wheat germ oil supplementation for sportsmen were carried out at Illinois in 1945 when it
was concluded that the height of the T wave of the electrocardiogram was increased, as was the speed of the Total Body
Reaction Jump. In later, more comprehensive experiments, it
was found that besides improvement in treadmill running
(susceptible to psychological 'will-power' effect) other objective

improvements were found after supplementation. The brachial pulse wave, indicative of greater circulatory fitness, was found to show improvement.

There was a convincing study by Cureton published in *Research Quarterly*, December 1955. Groups of men were matched on the basis of treadmill running time. The experimental group fed on wheat germ oil concentrate improved over six weeks from 3.44 to 5.14 minutes on an all-out treadmill run. The control group, despite an age advantage but fed on lard placebos, improved with the *same* amount of training, but *no* extra vitamin, only from 3.34 to 4.06 minutes. The differences in improvement in the two groups were statistically significant. The men did not know what they were taking except that *both* groups thought it was 'vitamins.'

An experiment by Dr Ershoff of the University of Southern California in 1955 involved guinea-pigs swimming completely to exhaustion, after which they sank. The guinea-pigs on wheat germ oil completely out-swam litter mates not fed wheat germ oil. In a later experiment it was shown that a group of guinea-pigs on a concentrated crystalline compound made from wheat germ oil averaged 70.4 minutes swimming time, compared with 57.7 minutes on wheat germ oil alone, 36.2 minutes on cotton seed oil and 40.3 minutes on basic control rations only. The differences due to wheat germ oil derivative and wheat germ oil were statistically highly significant.

Bernauer[17] with Illinois University runners found that the brachial pulse waves of the treated subjects improved more than the untreated. It was interesting that the two outstanding male swimmers in the 1956 American team, George Breen and Bill Yorzyk (both of whom became Olympic record-holders) were the only members of the male team to use wheat germ oil systematically.

Cureton[18] said that the wide use of vitamin E by the Australian Swimming Team in training for the 1956 Olympic Games 'has been credited in part for Australia's outstanding success.' Certainly all members of the Australian team *were* taking large quantities of vitamin E, even up to 1,500 mg. per day!

Objective evidence in favour of using vitamin E, such as improvement in brachial pulse wave, electrocardiogram and other physiological measurements, as well as improvement in

85 SWIMMERS AND VITAMIN PILLS

actual performance, is difficult to refute.

Objective improvement in cardiac function has been shown when vitamin E is taken *in conjunction with training*. This may be the key to the problem of why there have been so many contradictory reports on the results of alpha tocopherol therapy in heart conditions. Alpha tocopherol possibly only carries out its beneficial effects of improving function when the organism is active.

Recently it has been claimed that vitamin E in large doses may cause fat to be deposited subcutaneously, but this has been reported in cases of relatively inactive subjects. In regard to toxicity it is interesting that E. V. Shute[16] reported that he had taken 200 mg. daily for twelve years and 400 mg. daily for eight years, without sign of ill effect.

I believe that scientific evidence favours beneficial effects of feeding swimmers in hard training with extra vitamins.

Therefore we recommend nutritious food *and* in addition extra vitamins for athletes in strenuous training.

REFERENCES

1. Beckman, H. (1958). Drugs. Their Nature, Action and Use. p. 635. W. B. Saunders & Co.
2. Bicknell, F. and Prescott, F. (1945). The Vitamins in Medicine. London. Heinemann.
3. Bourne, G. H. (1948). Vitamins and Muscular Exercise. *British Journal of Nutrition*, Vol. 2, No. 3, p. 261.
4. Gounelle, H. (1940). *Bull. Soc. Med. Hosp.* Paris, 56, 225.
5. McCormick, W. J. (1940). *Med. Rec.*, 152, 439.
6. Doroschuk, E. U. and Cureton, T. K. (1960). *Nadbitka Autorshka*, Vol. 3.
7. Lauschner, E. (1956). The Works Doctor and Large-Scale Catering Experience in Remote Large Construction Works in High Mountains. *Helv. Med. Acta*, 23: 240–267.
8. Selye, H. (1937). *Endocrinology*, 21, p. 169.
9. Sayers, H. (1945). *Endocrinology*, 37, p. 96.
10. Dugal, L. and Therian, J. (1949). *Endocrinology*, 44, p. 420.
11. Baccus, H. and Toompas, C. L. (1951). *Science*, 113, p. 269.
12. Harris, L. J. and Ray, S. M. (1933). *Biochem. J.*, 27, p. 303.
13. Bantwell, J. (1950). *J. Applied Phys.*, 2, p. 388.
14. Pirani, C. L. (1952). *Metabolism*, 1, p. 197.

15. Forbes Carlile (1951). Evidence of Low Ascorbic Acid Levels in Young Swimmers. Part of unpublished M.Sc. thesis, University of Sydney.
16. Shute, E. V. (1958). The Summary, 10, No. 1.
17. Bernauer, E. (1956). Unpublished work on file at the University of Illinois.
18. Cureton, T. K. (1957). Observations at Melbourne. *Swimming Age*. Vol. 31, p. 87.

CHAPTER EIGHT

Stress and Strain

EVEN the most modern books and articles on coaching methods cannot tell us much of a scientific nature about how best to train. What solid facts there are enable us to do little more than *guess* why one athlete makes his personal best time while another, working on exactly the same training programme, may fail to perform anywhere near his previous best. As Professor A. V. Hill says in his article in the *Encyclopaedia Britannica* (1950 Edition), 'There is very little physiological knowledge about the changes which come over the body in physical training.'

The guiding lights for many coaches have been the methods used by the reigning champion and the most successful trainers, and, admittedly, with rule-of-thumb methods some progress seems to have been made. For instance it is now generally accepted that for maximum possible performance an athlete must train for hours rather than minutes a day, and the 'fast-slow' training principle first used by the Swedish runners in the 1930s is now widely and successfully practised in many sports. Yet we are still very much in the dark as to the *best* way to train, because the various methods of training have not yet been evaluated scientifically.

It is not difficult to find the reason for this lack of knowledge about training. The human body is a complex organism with so many physiological, psychological and social factors, all interacting, that it is both difficult and time-consuming to make well-controlled experiments, holding enough variable factors constant, to come to many definite conclusions. Nowadays, civilised society holds the opinion that striving for athletic honours *is* a worthy goal at least for some of its members, and this provides reason enough for the scientist and physical educator to be curious about the basic principles governing strenuous physical performance. There will have to be many observations and experiments with the 'whole' athlete in his own particular sphere of physical performance, if there is to be real progress in solving the problem of training an athlete to perform at his best. Experiments with guinea-pigs and other animals whose physiologies are similar to man's, although useful at times, will not tell us the *whole* story.

We must carefully observe human beings during hard physical training so that scientific ideas can be established on which coaches can base their training methods.

The Stress Concept

It has been accepted for some time that internal and external stresses play an important part in determining the health of man. As you read this you will see that, in training the swimmer, we should be much concerned with the story of stress, because exercise in itself is a considerable stress. It has long been realised that assaults by physical violence, microbes and disease, climatic conditions and nervous tension constitute common human stresses. As Stewart Wolf, a famous New York psychiatrist, pointed out, nervous strain alone, represented by threats and conflicts, real or imaginary, conscious or unconscious, constitutes a large portion of the stress to which man is continually exposed.

There is now much evidence showing that stress can cause general malfunction of bodily processes. Various biological mechanisms have been shown to be concerned in this response to stress.

Many workers have contributed to what is known as the Stress Concept, particularly regarding the effect of the emotions on bodily disease. Dr Hans Selye, experimenting mainly with rats, rabbits and guinea-pigs, has been able to demonstrate definite reproducible effects on the animal organism from a *wide variety* of stresses. This Canadian's research has taught us something of the mechanism by which bodily changes of stress are brought about. Selye spotlighted the anterior pituitary gland (about the size of a pea, almost in the centre of the head) and adrenal cortex glands (situated on top of the kidneys) as playing parts in what he called the General Adaptation Syndrome. A Syndrome may be defined as a *complex of symptoms*.

A stream-lined champion is 12-year-old Ryde swimmer Gillian de Greenlaw. Gillian established herself in 1963 as a potential 'great' when she won the Australian Junior Championship 110 yards Butterfly (long course) and recorded 1 minute 13.6 seconds in the heat. She also won the 220 yards Junior Butterfly in the excellent time of 2 minutes 47.8 seconds. Gillian trains at all styles; at 12 she swum the 440 yards medley in 6 minutes 4 seconds, 440 yards freestyle in 5 minutes 22 seconds, the 55 yards backstroke in 35.1 seconds and 55 yards butterfly in 33.1 seconds. At 13 she became Australia's youngest Olympian.

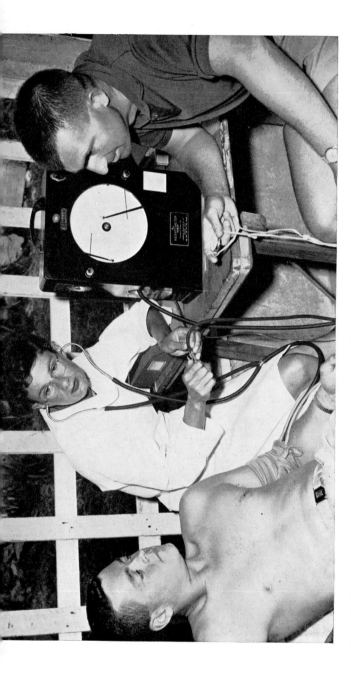

My wife Ursula and I make a Heartometer test on our pupil Terry Gathercole, who at the time held three world breast-stroke records. The pulsations from the blood pressure cuff around Terry's arm are recorded as an ink tracing on the circular graph paper. During hard training there is a gradual improvement in the size and quality of the pulse waves due to an increase in the power of the heart beat.

The General Adaptation Syndrome

Hans Selye has shown that such stressing agents as infections, poisons, trauma from burns or mechanical damage, heat, cold, starvation and MUSCULAR FATIGUE as well as having their own quite definite specific actions on a part of the organism, also invariably have generalised and *non-specific* effects on the whole body, *superimposed* upon all the specific effects. Please re-read this important idea.

The outstanding common effects of prolonged stress which Selye reported with experimental animals were –

1. Enlargement of the adrenal cortex gland and cellular changes there, indicative of increased glandular activity.
2. General atrophy of the lymph glands with concomitant changes in the blood cell count, particularly in respect of the eosinophil blood cells and lymphocytes.
3. Erosions and ulcers in the gastro-intestinal tract.

These and other changes are characteristic of what Selye called the *General Adaptation Syndrome* (*the G.A.S.*).

Under the influence of various stressing agents, including muscular exertion which can be an important stressor, the body changes in such a way as to adapt itself. According to Selye this *adaptation* can be differentiated into three stages –

(i) The Alarm Reaction. (Shock and Counter-shock.)
(ii) The State of Resistance.
(iii) The Stage of Exhaustion.

The *Alarm Reaction* is sub-divided into two stages, shock and counter-shock. Shock represents the organism's initial response when suddenly exposed to stimuli to which the organism is either quantitatively or qualitatively *not* adapted. For example, an animal may be in a state of training for muscular exercise. For this animal, running on a treadmill for five minutes may cause only a very mild G.A.S., but the totally untrained litter-mate may show a very marked response. However, if the stress is severe enough even the animal which has been trained to withstand it will show *some* Alarm Reaction changes.

The changes which occur in shock include diminished blood pressure, loss of muscle tone, a sustained very high heart-rate and, if the stress is very severe and prolonged, gastro-intestinal ulceration. However, with mild stresses (and usually exercise only acts as a mild stress), the main signs are merely transient high heart-rate and some chemical and cellular changes in the constitution of the blood.

As Selye pointed out, muscular exercise as a stress gives a 'minimum of shock and a maximum of counter-shock.' Exercise which causes very little tissue damage precipitates an almost pure G.A.S. response.

In the stage of counter-shock the physiological changes of shock become generally reversed, i.e. blood pressure rises above normal, and soon it seems that the adaptive mechanisms of the body proceed at a greater rate than the destructive processes. Adaptation occurs when, because of exposure to stress, an organism shows an increased capacity to resist that stress.

During the period of counter-shock there is an increased rate of adaptive processes. The organism becomes active, shows evidence of increased psychic stimulation and carries out activities denoting a sense of wellbeing. Physiological changes occur including lymph gland atrophy and a lowered eosinophil cell blood count.

Resistance to *all* stress, including the stress which precipitated the reaction, is *low* during shock but during counter-shock resistance to all stresses is *increased*. However, the protection, called cross-resistance, of the counter-shock reaction is temporary. If the precipitating stress is continued, the animal goes into what Selye calls the *Stage of Resistance* when there is increased resistance only for that particular stress, and decreased resistance for *all other stresses*.

In the *Stage of Resistance* the organism will continue to resist the original stressing agent but it becomes *more vulnerable* to *other* stresses which, in addition to the original stress, if severe enough, may each be capable of producing another Alarm Reaction (on top of the Resistance reactions which have already occurred).

The final stage of the G.A.S. is the *Stage of Exhaustion*, typified by non-specific detrimental reactions resulting from prolonged over-exposure to one or more stimuli to which adaptation had occurred but can now no longer be maintained. During the Exhaustion Stage, resistance to *all* stressing agents is lowered and any stress may precipitate a violent reaction of prolonged shock and death.

The passage of the animal from one stage into another is usually a gradual one and it is not always easy to recognise the stage. There seems little doubt, both experimentally and in practice, that resistance to all stresses *decreases* gradually as the Stage of Exhaustion is approached.

Selye pointed out many times in his papers that practically nothing is known about the physiological changes occurring as the animal progresses from a state of resistance towards exhaustion. Even less is known about *human responses* (e.g. a swimmer forced with training into a State of Exhaustion). Our observations made on the 1960 Australian Olympic team training in Townsville throw some light on this subject. The results are summarised in the following chapter.

By way of graphic illustration of the G.A.S. response to cold as a stressing agent it may be of interest to re-tell Selye's story of what happened to mice taken from a mild room temperature and placed in a freezing chamber.

When taken from the room at about 70° F. and placed in an environment close to freezing point, the mice at first became prostrated with shock. They then started to run about and carry on their normal activities, at first appearing overactive (the counter-shock phase) and then apparently passing into the State of Resistance when it was difficult to tell the difference between them and mice living under normal conditions. After some hours, one by one the mice began to succumb, becoming sluggish in their activity and finally dying of shock.

Those who have observed athletes during training will by now be able to discern that the Selye G.A.S. 'cap' fits in many places. I feel that the swimmer when trained hard almost invariably shows many responses of the G.A.S. described by Selye. Superficially it is often difficult to recognise a state close to exhaustion.

Selye postulated that the animal organism (including man) has a finite, *limited Adaptation Energy.* However, as Selye points out, this concept is an abstraction in-so-far as we do not yet know the *exact* nature of Adaptation Energy. All we can say at present is that the body does respond as *though* it had just such a limited supply. The facts advanced by Hans Selye, with my own observations on myself and on other subjects in severe training, support the concept that all stress effects are *summated* and draw on this limited Adaptation Energy of the individual.

Some individuals can always be observed to be able to stand distinctly more training than others, and continue to show improvement. Whatever may be the reason for this, no doubt there are hereditary constitutional differences, the fact remains that only the naïve coach would dispense a rigid system of written training instructions to be carried out 'regardless.' Bitter experience has shown many times, that what is one person's training 'meat' might well be another's poison. As far as possible each swimmer must be treated as an individual when dosing out training mileage.

The particular aim of swimming training is to stimulate the body to adapt itself in a specific way by continuously repeating physical exercise of a specialised nature. Nowadays with the rewards and prestige for sporting success more numerous, harmful effects from the stress of physical exercise become a more likely condition than in the past. High training mileage, at any cost, has become almost an obsession with many of today's swimmers and coaches.

Selye's concept that the body has a limited quantity of Adaptation Energy, and that stresses should be summated when considering their effects on the organism, he has stated to be *the most important thing he learned* from his extensive research into stress.

When an organism suffers chronic exposure to a particular stress, the result is an increase in resistance to that stress and a reduction in the non-specific resistance to *other* stresses. The importance of this for the swimmer is apparent. The highly trained individual may withstand a relatively great load of a particular exercise for which he has been trained, but succumbs more easily than the normal healthy person to *other* stressing agents, such as bacterial infection.

Any stress, including muscular exercise whether major or minor, according to Selye draws on the bank of Adaptation Energy, but it is the stresses for which the individual is less well adapted that will make the greatest physical demands and be most likely to hasten exhaustion reactions.

Stresses on the Swimmer in Training

For the swimmer there are two important questions arising from the G.A.S. (General Adaptation Syndrome). First, what are the main stresses which may make a demand on his powers of adaptation, and second, what signs and symptoms are indicative of a failing store of Adaptation Energy?

In answer to the first question, here is a list of possible stresses:

    (i) Muscular exercise.
    (ii) Dietary inadequacy.
    (iii) Climatic conditions.
    (iv) Bacterial infections and disease.
    (v) Emotional conflict and unrest.
    (vi) Insufficient rest and sleep.
    (vii) Miscellaneous stress – everyday wear and tear of living.

(i) Even when everything seems ideal for a swimmer's training, it is still possible to overload the athlete with too much or too intensive a training programme. Obviously the best general practice should always to be increase the training load *gradually*, giving the body time to make its changes of adaptation. I believe that a common reason for failure of swimmers is over-enthusiastically starting off on a training programme which is too severe. Training should be increased gradually, not only in the one season, but also year by year.

Exercise, according to the G.A.S. theory, causes an Alarm Reaction with an emphasis on the (beneficial) counter-shock stage. During this stage the individual, misled by his feeling of well-being, may continue to exercise *very* hard even though his general powers of adaptation will then be low and he may be fast travelling towards the Stage of Exhaustion.

A top swimmer in hard training is often in an early stage of resistance, sometimes he may push himself on too far into this stage so that his adaptation energy nears its limit – then suddenly, a stress (not even very severe) such as a race or time trial may prove the last straw to his load – he will have reached the stage of exhaustion.

(ii) A diet may be completely satisfactory for the relatively inactive person, but may not contain the necessary quantity of nutrients, particularly vitamins, for a person doing very strenuous training. There seems fairly good evidence now that in the diets of many individuals stressed with exercise there are insufficient amounts of vitamin C and vitamin B complex. Moreover, it is conceivable that there exist personal idiosyncrasies for optimum performance. Individuals may need differing amounts of certain vitamins, some much more than others.

(iii) For the swimmer practising in outdoor pools, cold can be a very significant stress.

(iv) Bacterial infection and disease may call for a great deal of Adaptation Energy. Added to the physical exertion of training, disease can easily precipitate early exhaustion. It is an ill-advised athlete who trains hard or races when he is unwell.

(v) The well adjusted and happy person will have a minimum of psychic unrest. Mental stress probably causes some effects on the body. The fact that emotional upsets can affect the body, and are associated with many types of physiological malfunction and diseases, certainly suggests strongly that the emotionally well-balanced swimmer, with an even temperament and the personality factors generally associated with being a 'good sport,' has an important advantage over the unhappy, restless individual who is kept busy dealing not only with battles in his field of competition but also with battles in himself.

(vi) Insufficient rest and sleep may be another stress decreasing Adaptation Energy and hindering maximum performance. A swimmer may be habitually having insufficient rest and be blaming his poor performances on everything except this fundamental need for more sleep. The athlete requires much more rest than the non-athlete.

(vii) Under the heading of miscellaneous stresses, many and various factors could be discussed. For instance, smoking may be a stress easily borne by an otherwise relatively non-stressed person, but to the swimmer such indulgence may be at an adaptation cost he cannot afford. The everyday wear and tear of living involving the athlete's occupation, his travelling to work, his hobbies, studies and not least his social obligations, are all performed at the cost of some energy of adaptation. Stock-taking of these activities should be made by all concerned in preparing an athlete. These everyday stresses, as well as the actual training itself, are of the utmost importance and should be carefully considered when planning a schedule and assessing reactions to training.

Signs and Symptoms of Strain

Our observations of athletes in severe training for a variety of sports have confirmed Selye's hypothesis that whether a person is ill from disease, or over-stressed by other means such as exercise, he tends to show the same general reactions.

Here is a short list of some signs and symptoms of failing adaptation:

    (i) Chronic loss of body weight.
   (ii) Joint and muscle pain not attributable to a particular local injury.
  (iii) Chronically occurring intestinal upsets.
  (iv) Swollen lymph glands (tonsils and inguinal glands of the groin).
   (v) Blocked nose and one-day cold (rhinitis).
  (vi) Skin rashes such as hives (urticaria).
 (vii) Psychological unrest, irritability, insomnia, general fatigue often referred to as 'staleness.'
(viii) General muscular tenseness.

Loss of weight in the swimmer who is training, whether or not it is accompanied by poor appetite, represents generally increased katabolism (destructive processes), which Selye says is characteristic of an advanced G.A.S. response. Some coaches and trainers of race-horses and greyhounds place considerable faith in the use of this sign as a guide. Once when visiting the Payne Whitney Gymnasium at the Yale University, I saw members of the American Swimming team under coach Bob Kiphuth carefully recording their stripped body weights on a chart. This was a daily practice.

Joint pains have for some time been recognised as a common symptom of various diseases. Such symptoms in the athlete in terms of the G.A.S. represent a state of strain. I had some personal experience in this regard. After several months' training for marathon running, when I had built up a fairly good specific adaptation to running long distances (demonstrated by improving time-trial performances), joint and muscle pains became a regular occurrence. When I disregarded these general pains and other symptoms, maintained the training load and ran in a marathon race, the result was nearly complete physical breakdown requiring six weeks in hospital.

During the stress of very hard training, I have often noticed, both in myself and in my pupils, swollen lymph glands in tonsils and groin area, and urticaria (hives). Almost immediate relief has always followed when the stress of muscular exercise has been removed.

Sleeplessness and nervous irritability are classical signs of the condition widely known as 'staleness.' It is my belief that this condition may often be understood in terms of the G.A.S. as the Stage of Exhaustion.

One may expect that other signs of an advanced G.A.S. will be observed and reported in the future, not only in experimental animals but also in humans. In people who are exercising strenuously, the G.A.S. signs will usually be uncomplicated by the specific effects of disease. This 'pure' G.A.S. response makes the study of the athlete of general scientific interest.

Just as lifting the stressing load relieves the exhausted experimental animal, so rest will restore the jaded, 'stale' athlete – but how much rest the over-trained athlete needs or whether there should be a *complete* rest from all training, are still matters of judgment – decisions which will remain in the category of coaching 'art' until we have gained more reliable knowledge.

The next challenge for the physiologist is to *detect and measure* the degree of strain in an individual. Not a great deal has been done in this field of research, although my wife and I have made observations along these lines. For instance, several athletes in training (including myself) who appeared to be in good general health, developed a condition which one would interpret as staleness. Haemoglobinuria (traces of compounds of blood in the urine) was often found immediately after training. Two athletes, members of the 1952 Australian Olympic team with haemoglobinuria (blood in urine) after efforts, acting on my advice took heed of this sign, and eased off their training considerably. They went on to register personal records and reach Olympic finals. It was interesting that when these athletes after a rest period of about a week started to train strenuously again the haemoglobinuria did not reappear. In other athletes who were obviously in a state of chronic fatigue, I have observed considerable changes from the normal in the count of blood eosinophil cells. Although no allergy or other illness could be detected, the count reached a very high level (from 600 to 1,000 per cu. mm. compared with a normal count of 50 to 100). This lasted over a period of a week or more. It looked very much like a measurable sign of strain. Other effects such as altered T waves of the electrocardiogram are considered in the following chapter on scientific testing.

Robert Windle illustrating the high-elbow technique of many present-day Australians. In January 1963 the Sydney swimmer established a new World Record for the 220 yards at 2 minutes 01.1 seconds and in April made a new World Record for 200 metres with 2 minutes 00.3 seconds. In 1963 Windle won the Australian 220, 440, 880 and 1,650 yards Championships and was beaten by a 'touch' by David Dixon in the 110 yards sprint, thus narrowly missing the honour of joining the list of famous Australian swimmers to win the clean sweep of Australian freestyle titles. This has been accomplished by Dick Cavill, Bill Longworth, John Marshall and John Konrads. Three months later (July 27, 1963) the 16-year-old American, Don Schoullander became the first to break the elusive 2-minute 'barrier' for the 200 metres. At Los Angeles he recorded 1 minute 58.8 seconds, replacing Windle's name on the world record list.

It is possible that there are many changes in addition to those already observed, which will act as indicators of strain, and show that Adaptation Energy is running out.

Even in our present state of knowledge, the astute coach is often aware of oncoming exhaustion and acts on the warning signs and symptoms *before* he drives the swimmer into a state from which he may take a long time to recover. Some of the changes mentioned above occur relatively early in the process, and prompt action by the coach in assessing the total stress load, and lightening it, can often save the situation.

Normally swimmers in training are in a relatively early stage of resistance. If the swimmer is pushed through the Resistance Stage, for a time he continues to increase his specific adaptation and potential maximum performance. Gradually the risk of straining increases as his general adaptation, and finally his specific adaptation, begin to be lost at a rapidly increasing rate. There is often a very thin line between training and *straining*. Vigilance and careful handling by the coach are essential if good performances are to be more than haphazard occurrences.

These pictures are stills from our 16 mm instructional film. They give you a good idea of what champion swimmers actually do.

(*Top left*) Dawn Fraser, from above water. The head is seen to have turned, with the cheek well down in the water as the breath is taken. Notice the elbow higher than the hand during the arm recovery.

(*Top right*) Dawn Fraser, from underwater. Dawn's hand follows an S-shaped 'feathering' path through the water. Notice that here the right forearm is well bent and that the hand is far across the central axis. Many top Australian swimmers have shown this characteristic of pulling across the centre line.

(*Middle left*) Dawn Fraser, from underwater. Notice that Dawn's left arm is about to press down on the central axis. Her right arm has practically finished its long pull back, the hand finishing at the *thigh*, not coming out at the hip.

(*Middle right*) Murray Rose, from underwater. Notice firstly the extent of the body roll when Murray turns to breathe, and secondly the beginning of the powerful whip-lash kick of his right leg. Even when he only uses a 2-beat kick, Murray gains much propulsion from his legs.

(*Bottom left*) David Theile, from underwater. Here David's horizontal body position is evident and also the bent arm pull which is seen in all the leading male backstrokers today.

(*Bottom right*) David Theile, from underwater. His hands enter the water ready to pull, a little wide of the shoulder. Following the final 'rotating action' of the forearm, the hand can be seen finishing well below the level of the thigh.

D

The training of an athlete is a great responsiblility because several of his very important possessions are being used – the athlete's time, his enthusiasm and his powers of adaptation to life stresses. Training the swimmer may be likened to bending a green twig. The body may eventually mould itself in response to the force of continuously imposed physical exercise, but a little too much stress of exercise and the body, like the twig, may be strained and reach its breaking point.

Rhythm has been named a characteristic of life. There is a time for strenuous activity and a time for resting. The severity of a too rigid training programme may easily drive the swimmer to exhaustion. The coach whose mind is obsessed with the idea that long distances and very hard training must be done at any cost may for a while seem to have successful results, but many of his pupils will invariably 'fall by the wayside' as they reach the limit of their Adaptation Energy. The coach may be compared with the violinist feeling for the right note. He must proceed directly and definitely, but at the same time listen carefully for the note he is producing. If his string has slackened slightly he must adjust his technique to meet the contingencies of the moment. The sensitive trainer, with a background of some scientific knowledge and experience, will feel his way carefully with various individuals. He will not be *too* rigid a task master and risk the 'twig snapping.'

Conclusions

Coaching swimmers will gradually become more scientific as our knowledge becomes more extensive and better organised but the 'art' will always lie in recognising personal idiosyncrasies and blending hard training with enough rest to give the optimum amounts of specific adaptation for each individual's Adaptation Energy.

No matter what modifications and extensions are eventually made to the Hans Selye concept, I believe that the theory of the General Adaptation Syndrome in its present form is of great value to the coach who is seeking a scientific basis on which to organise his observations of the effect of training.

As Selye has said, 'Our facts must be correct; our theories need not be if they help us discover important new facts.'

CHAPTER NINE

Testing Swimmers in the Laboratory

IF it is possible to over-stress the swimmer with severe training
and to bring on a state of strain as suggested in the last chapter,
then it should be possible to measure objectively the signs of
strain with physiological testing methods (i.e. by measuring
changes in the body functions). With this as a basic premise, a
number of years ago I began making various tests on swimmers
during their period of hard training. Later my wife Ursula joined
me in this work – in fact in recent years she has carried out practically all the testing of swimmers in the Professor Cotton
Memorial Laboratory we have set up for this purpose.

It is obviously important to know whether, and to what
extent, a swimmer or any other athlete is in a state of physiological strain during training. When we can test for strain we are
in a position to take appropriate action and perhaps prevent
over-training and greatly worsened performances.

The best way of explaining something of this work, without
becoming too detailed or too technical, may be to reproduce
here a summary of a scientific paper we wrote after conducting a
long-term series of tests on the 1960 Australian Olympic team
during their training at Townsville in Northern Queensland.

Here is this summary of the testing work as it was presented
in a paper read at the National Coaching Forum in Sydney in
1961.

A Summary of Interpretations and Applications of Physiological
Testing on the Australian Olympic Swimmers in Hard Training.
by Forbes Carlile, M.Sc.(Sydney)
and Ursula Carlile, Dip.Phys.Ed.(Adelaide)

INTRODUCTION
During the eight weeks hard training period (June 20 to
August 12, 1960) carried out in Townsville (North Queensland)

99

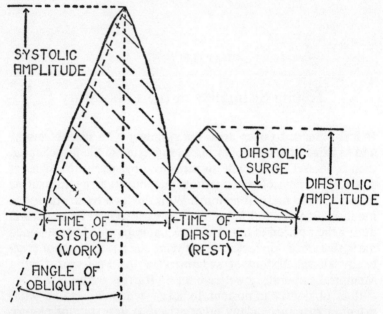

Fig. 2—A Pulse Wave. This is a diagramatic enlargement of a tracing made on the Heartometer (shown in picture opposite page 89). This tracing represents the result of *one* heart beat.

before the Rome Olympic Games, twenty-eight Australian swimmers were subjected each week to a series of physiological tests. The data was collected with the co-operation of the swimmers, coaches and the Amateur Swimming Union of Australia.

The detailed results of this work are published in the *Australian Journal of Physical Education*, October-November 1961. It is our intention here only to summarise the most significant aspects of the results and to discuss their implications on the training of swimmers.

THE BRACHIAL PULSE WAVE

The brachial pulse wave was taken from an inflated blood pressure cuff on the upper arm. Tracings were made with the Cameron Heartometer. Various characteristics of the wave, such as area and height, are known to reflect the capacity of the heart and circulation for endurance activity. (See Fig. 2.)

From the measurements of six characteristics of the brachial pulse wave known to be associated with circulatory fitness, an average standard score was calculated for each swimmer. The tables used for comparison were originally drawn up by Professor T. K. Cureton, from a group of healthy but untrained male college students. A score of 50 means that a subject would rank half way in a group of 100 average young males.

At the beginning of the hard training period the average score for the sixteen male swimmers was 55 and for the twelve females 46 (comparing with the same male standard).

After eight weeks of severe training (up to seven miles in a day) the average score for the males had risen to 83 and for the females to 68. This was a substantial improvement.

The single characteristic of the brachial pulse wave which showed the greatest and most consistent change with training was the ratio of resting time of the heart to working time. Twenty-seven swimmers showed an increase in this ratio and one remained unchanged. The average increase in rest-work ratio for the twenty-eight swimmers was 70% (from 0.17 to 0.29) after the eight weeks of training.

Another marked change with training was in the appearance of the diastolic surge (or rebound wave). A large diastolic surge indicates a combination of forceful heart action and an elastic rebound of resilient blood vessels. The overall average increased from 0.02 mm. to 1.6 mm. Twenty-five swimmers increased in this measurement, three remained unchanged in this, but improved in other characteristics of the pulse wave.

DISCUSSION

The differences in the brachial pulse wave due to training give us an objective method of assessing with comparative ease changes in the circulatory efficiency of individuals.

It is remarkable that the sixteen champion male swimmers at the beginning of hard training averaged a score of 55, only five standard scores above average college males. This was in spite of the fact that the swimmers had been in peak racing form only three months previously and, for two months before we tested them, had been carrying out weight training and general calisthenics for up to five hours a week. With the hard endurance training in eight weeks at Townsville the male swimmers improved by an average of 28 standard scores and the females by

22 standard scores.

These results indicate that weight training, even when carried out energetically and consistently, does not result in any great improvement in circulatory efficiency and, in this case, was not enough even to *maintain* the circulatory fitness which the swimmers showed in February (four months previously), when they were at their physical peak for swimming and gained selection for the team. It was interesting that three months without swimming training could apparently result in such a fall-off in circulatory efficiency. One would have expected a very much greater carry-over for such a comparatively short time.

Previously *untrained* individuals could not be expected to improve as the swimmers did in eight weeks. Ordinary individuals without a background of hard training would almost certainly be unable to stand up to such intensive training.

Despite their advance in circulatory fitness, for at least six of the eight weeks there was little or no improvement in some of the swimmers' time-trial performances. This at first sight is very puzzling. We interpret this as indicating that although the intense physical exercise improved the cardiovascular system, the effort involved in doing this caused something in the nature of a nervous depletion. With more rest during the 'tapering-off' period the nervous system would seem to regenerate *before* the cardiovascular fitness has deteriorated to any great extent, and thus a peak performance is possible.

There is some objective evidence for this 'nervous depletion' theory. If severely exercised rats are killed, and stained sections are made of their brain tissue, microscopic nissyl bodies present in the nerve cells of rested rats will have disappeared. This probably indicates that other so far undetected changes, as well as those in the cells of the nervous system, might be caused by severe effort and repetitive muscular action.

From common observation, individuals require different general preparation and tapering-off programmes to reach their peak, at which time the combination of circulatory efficiency and nervous repletion is at an optimum.

It should be noted that factors which may be termed 'psychological' are *not* involved in the above consideration. Obviously emotional factors *can* play an important part in physical performance, but fatigue of the nervous system by over-use is a different matter. The condition known as 'staleness' probably involves mainly actual physical changes in the nervous and circulatory systems.

It was possible to make an indirect comparison with two previously very successful swimming teams, the Americans of 1948 and the Japanese of 1936. The Australian male swimmers, judged by their brachial pulse waves, were clearly superior in cardiovascular efficiency to both. This was probably due in large part to the fact that the Australians in 1960, with modern interval training methods, trained harder and longer than swimmers had before. It is of course, difficult to assess the effect that natural ability and technique had on the Australians' performances.

The practical application of the study of the brachial pulse wave during training is that the degree of circulatory fitness of an individual can be assessed at any stage by observing partcularly the diastolic surge (the magnitude of the rebound wave) or even better by calculating the rest-to-work ratio of the heart. These two factors show marked changes with increased fitness. The other important conclusion is that we cannot expect weight training to contribute in any large part to *circulatory* efficiency.

BLOOD PRESSURE

We found that the average resting systolic (maximum) brachial blood pressure of the male swimmers *increased* gradually from 116 mm. to 126 mm. in the eight weeks; the females increased only about 3 mm. from an average of 106 mm.

Fortunately, at rest no particularly high systolic blood pressures were discovered. Anything over 145 or 150 mm. would have been suggestive of either physiological strain caused by over-training, or of a pathological hypertensive state, requiring medical attention and even a complete lay-off from hard training.

The rising systolic blood pressure is possibly an indication of the increased force of each heart beat and may be interpreted as an indication of increased physiological adaptation.

Accompanying increase in systolic pressure both the males and females showed distinct *falls* during the eight weeks in their diastolic (minimum) blood pressures, the males falling from an average of 70 mm. to 61 mm., and the females from 68 mm to 63 mm.

The normal lying diastolic pressure is generally accepted as 75 or 80 mm. – about the same as we found in the swimmers before hard training. The fall in diastolic blood pressure with training was further evidence that after three months without swimming training cardiovascular fitness was only about equal to that of the average person.

With the hard training the significant and distinct fall in the resting diastolic blood pressure and the rise in systolic blood pressure would appear to be good indications of physiological adjustment to severe exercise.

The graphs showing the change in average resting blood pressures of the swimmers, over each of the eight weeks are shown in Fig. 3.

The diastolic response after thirty seconds vigorous running-on-the-spot was of particular interest. In recent years Cureton in the U.S.A. and Letounov of the U.S.S.R. have observed, contrary to previous ideas, that after exercise the normal response in a trained sportsman is a moderate fall in diastolic blood pressure immediately after the exercise, gradually returning to the resting level. When the average diastolic pressures of the swimmers were taken half a minute after the standard exercise, a gradual *decrease* in this average reading was found, in the males from 64 mm. in Week 1 to 50 mm. in Week 6. Later the fall was to 46 mm during Weeks 7 and 8.

The results for the female swimmers were similar.

The conclusion is drawn that this fall in diastolic blood pressure after exercise represents a physiological adaptation to training due, possibly, to greater vascular resiliency and the opening of blood vessels in the capilliary bed. This facilitates the movement of blood to the muscles.

There was very little further fall from Week 6 to Week 8 and this seems to indicate that most circulatory adjustment to severe exercise can be attained in about six weeks, at least by experienced swimmers in hard training.

It would not, however, be valid to decide on this evidence alone that six or even eight weeks' training is sufficient for swimmers to reach top form, because other physiological factors are also involved. We do not yet have the complete answer to

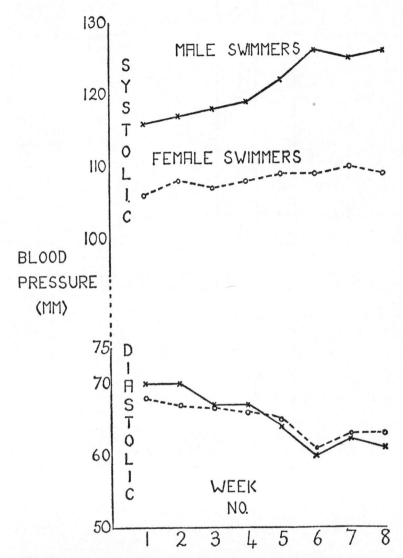

Fig. 3—This shows the steady average increase in resting systolic (maximum) blood pressure and the decrease in resting diastolic (minimum) blood pressure during the period of hard training. These changes are interpreted as indicating an adaptation response to hard physical exercise.

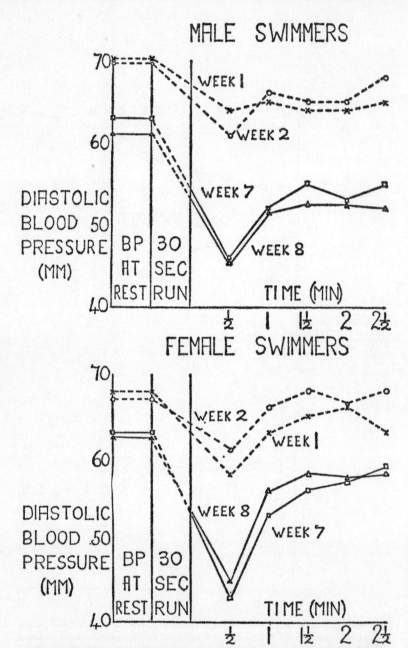

Fig. 4—After 30 seconds fast running on the spot the diastolic (minimum) blood pressure was recorded for 2½ minutes. Here it can be seen that the average for both the male and female swimmers showed a considerable fall between the first two weeks and the final weeks of hard training. This is interpreted as a favourable adaptive response to training and suggests a relatively simple physiological method of checking a swimmer's progress.

this problem of the optimum time required for training. No doubt this varies with individuals.

The average blood pressures for the whole group recorded after the standard exercise for each of the eight weeks are shown in Fig. 4.

An investigation of blood pressure changes for *individual* swimmers resulted in some interesting findings (see Figures 5 and 6). The diastolic pressure after exercise of Murray Rose, the eventual winner of the 400 metres at Rome, showed a gradual fall. After eight weeks it went as low as 20 mm.! He appeared on all criteria to be adjusting particularly well to his training. On the other hand John Monckton, who at the time held the world back-stroke record, showed *no* such diastolic fall in the eight weeks. On practically all criteria John Monckton was *not* adjusting favourably to his training load and was recording very poor trial times throughout the training period.

The practical application of this discovery of progressive diastolic blood pressure changes during training is that we have another way of measuring the degree of circulatory adjustment.

BODY WEIGHT

Loss of body weight during hard training is generally accepted as indicative of failing adaptation and strain.

The male swimmers maintained exactly the same average weight of 173 pounds throughout the eight weeks whilst the females showed a steady *increase* from an average 144 pounds to 147 pounds.

There were no spectacular changes in weight in the males but two girls, Ilsa Konrads and Ruth Everuss, urged by their coach, went on to a carbohydrate-low diet and both lost 8 lb in a week. However, this reduction was not sustained and the girls were soon back close to their original weights.

BLOOD HAEMOGLOBIN LEVEL

We have found in previous studies of sportsmen in hard training that drops of up to 20% in blood haemoglobin have occurred, invariably accompanied by relatively poor performances.

Apart from a deficiency of iron or other food substances necessary for the production of haemoglobin in the body,

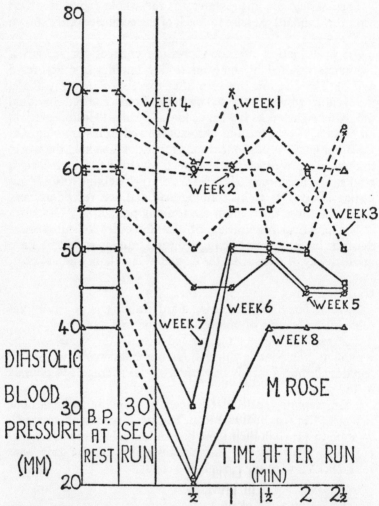

DIASTOLIC
BLOOD
PRESSURE
(MM)

80
70
60
50
40
30
20

B. P.
AT
REST

30
SEC
RUN

WEEK 4
WEEK 1
WEEK 2
WEEK 3
WEEK 7
WEEK 6
WEEK 5
WEEK 8

M. ROSE

TIME AFTER RUN
(MIN)

½ 1 1½ 2 2½

Fig. 5—Graph for M. Rose: this shows the individual response of one swimmer's diastolic blood pressure after the 30 second run on the spot. Murray responded well to the training and went on to win the Olympic 400 m event. Each week of training saw his diastolic blood pressure become gradually lower. Compare this response with that of John Monckton in the next diagram.

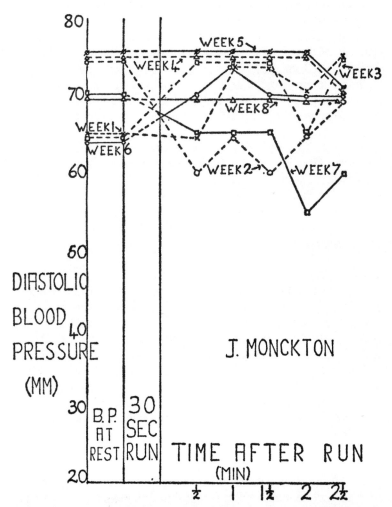

Fig. 6—Graph for J. Monckton: drawn to the same scale as Murray Rose's graph (Fig. 5). It can be seen that there was practically no decrease in backstroker John Monckton's diastolic blood pressure response after 30 seconds running exercise throughout the 8 weeks. This is interpreted as indicating poor adaptation to hard training. John performed poorly and was seldom well during the hard training period.

physiological strain of a chronic nature can result in reduced values.

Both male and female swimmers at Townsville were remarkably constant in their haemoglobin levels. The male average over the eight weeks varied between 15.5 and 15.6 gm. per 100 c.c. of blood. (The average value for N.S.W. males has been given as 15.7 gm.%.)

The average for the female swimmers over the eight weeks varied only between 14.0 and 14.2 gm. per 100 c.c. of blood. (The average value of N.S.W. females has been reported as 13.9 gm.%.)

The diets of the swimmers were completely adequate in all respects. They had a wide variety of natural foods and vitamin and mineral supplementation.

None of the twenty-eight swimmers during hard training was at any time found to have a physiologically abnormal haemoglobin level even when on *other* criteria some may have appeared to be in a state of strain.

PERSONALITY TRAITS

The Sixteen Personality Factor Questionnaire of R. Cattell, involving 374 questions, was used. The swimmers were scored on sixteen standard personality traits such as general intelligence, emotional stability, general neuroticism, etc. Such traits are recognised as a result of general psychological research.

The average scores of the complete group of twenty-eight swimmers showed very little difference from the average of the general population. However, there was a tendency for the group as a whole to score high in the factor indicative of being *demanding*, *excitable* and *impatient*, as compared with the characteristic, 'emotionally mature.'

When the results of eight male swimmers who were over 19 years of age were considered as a separate group, they scored high in 'independent self-sufficiency' and their scores indicated a strong control of emotion and general behaviour. These eight older males scored low in the factor indicating general nervous tension, a result one would expect to find in outstanding competitive sportsmen.

Reliable information on the personality of swimmers can obviously be of practical value to the coach by helping him understand his pupil, indicating how he or she should be handled. The subjective summing-up of the personality of another is often at best a rough guide, and, in fact, may be misleading because one's own personality structure influences judgment.

Perhaps in the future, for the guidance of competitive sportsmen, reliable psychological measurements coupled with interpretation by an expert will prove of importance.

THE ELECTROCARDIOGRAM

The electrocardiogram is a graphic record of very small electrical changes associated with each heart beat.

Abnormal T Waves of the E.C.G. have been demonstrated by the author as being associated with worsened performance and subjective feelings of fatigue. Both in this present study of Australian swimmers and with other sportsmen, T waves have been found which were so abnormal that expert cardiologists said that for ordinary people not in training, such records would cause the diagnosis of a serious heart condition, necessitating complete abandonment of strenuous activity. Most of the specialist physicians who were asked their opinion expressed great surprise at such abnormalities.

In the swimmers at Townsville it was found that the height of the largest wave of the complex, the so-called R wave, increased during the eight weeks by 24% in the males and 31% in the female swimmers. It may be concluded that as the heart becomes trained for strenuous activity and each contraction becomes more powerful, the R wave increases in height.

Referring again to the T wave changes that occurred, it may be said that in the Australian swimmers at Townsville when marked T wave distortion was found, invariably training times and time-trial performances were poor and the swimmers reported feeling unwell. Although most showed some reduction in height of the T waves and some flattening (see Fig. 7 and Fig. 8), eight of the 28 swimmers showed what might be regarded as *gross* distortions of this wave during the hard training, but it should also be stated that five or six other swimmers who showed generally poor progress in training had relatively normal electrocardiographs. The conclusion which we must draw from this is that the E.C.G. can measure only one aspect of fitness and that there can be other 'weak links' in the body's physiology

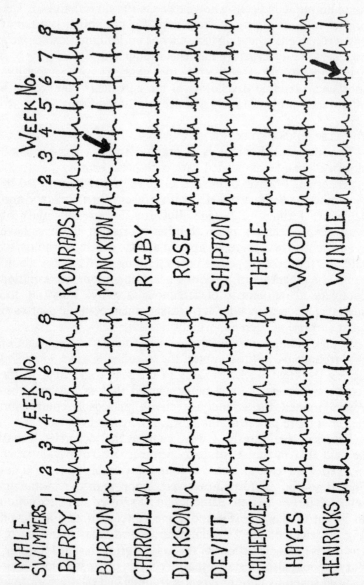

Fig. 7—Electrocardiograms. During the 8 weeks of hard training distortion of the 'T wave' was a common occurrence when swimmers were performing poorly and not feeling well. This was particularly noted in the cases of John Monckton and Robert Windle (see text).

which cannot be thus detected. No *single* test is satisfactory in itself for detecting physiological strain.

The swimmers who had T waves that were greatly distorted included Robert Windle, John Monckton and Alva Colquhoun. All three swimmers, during their training at Townsville, caused the team manager and their coaches great concern, on account of their poor trial times and the swimmers' subjective reports of how badly they felt.

Windle at 15 years of age had recorded 4 min. 33.3 sec. and 18-8.5 for 440 yards and 1,650 yards at the selection trials in January. When his T wave records were very distorted during Weeks 4, 5 and 6 (see Fig. 7) his trial times in Townsville were 4-51.5, 4-47.5 and 4-51.8. Immediately after his 4-51.8 time trial early in Week 6, Windle was forced to spend five days in bed with a respiratory infection, following this he swam an encouraging 4-36 and 18-28 in the official trials. At this stage, his electrocardiogram was normal again. Had he been given the opportunity to swim at the Olympic Games two weeks later (Rose and Konrads represented Australia) there were good indications that Windle would have been near his best.

John Monckton gave a similar story. Accompanying badly deformed T waves (see Fig. 7) his trial times for 110 yards back-stroke were more than five seconds outside his best. He felt unfit, complaining of tiredness and weakness.

With six days of very easy swimming before the end of Week 8 he had improved considerably in time trials, subjective feelings of fitness, *and* in T wave appearance. At Rome, if he had not badly misjudged his turn in the back-stroke final, Monckton almost certainly would have been within a second or two of his world record.

Alva Colquhoun, a sprinter who had a history of 'not being able to take hard training' had the most deformed T waves of any of the swimmers (see Fig. 8). They were diphasic and inverted on all leads (clinically a very serious condition), from after the first week at Townsville. Alva Colquhoun had gained team selection in February with 64.1 seconds for the 110 yards but her official trials in August were 66.2 and 66.1 with very distorted T waves. Almost continually during training she suffered from various illnesses – sinus infection, 'sore shoulders' and very painful and disabling 'fibrositis' in the back. She complained

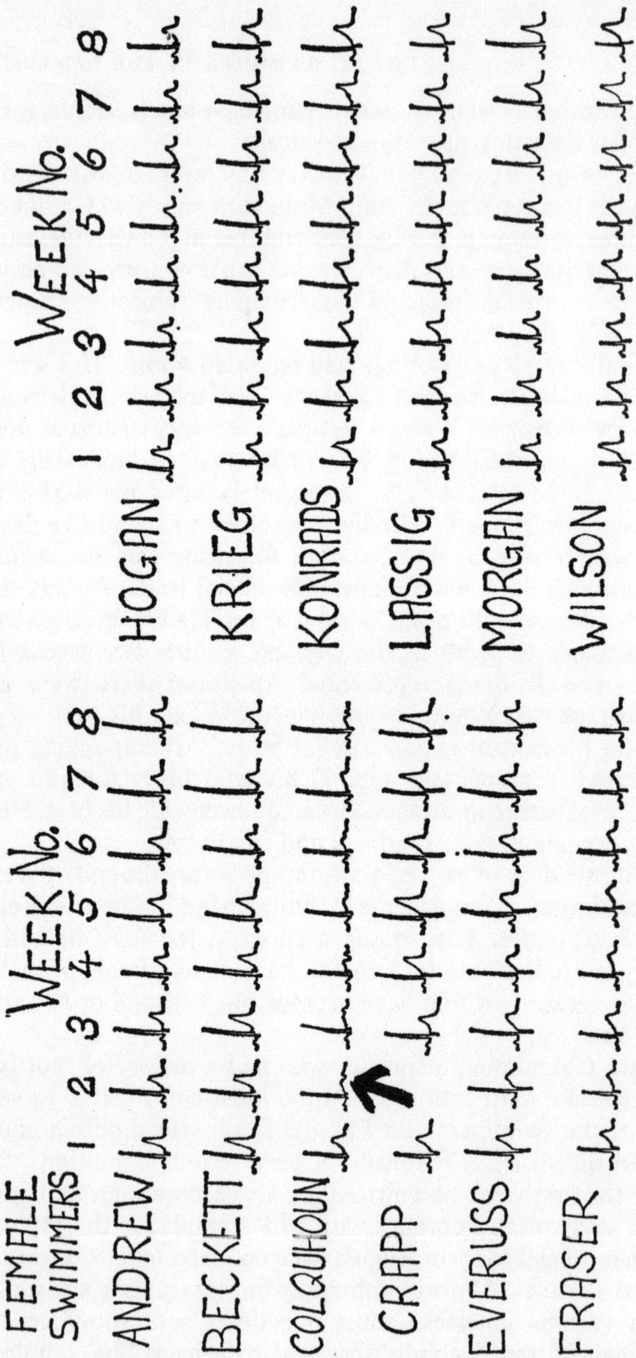

Fig. 8—The outstanding change in the 'T wave' of the Electrocardiogram was seen amongst the girls in Alva Colquhoun. For a discussion of this see the text.

week after week of joint pains and of feeling 'tired all over.'

With between two and three weeks' light preparation before her races at Rome – it being difficult during this period for the team to train for long sessions – her times were 62.5 and 62.8 for the 100 m in relay events. These times were within half a second of her personal best ever.

Discussion

This is possibly the first time that serial observations have been made on swimmers so heavily stressed with training.

The general consensus of expert medical opinion was that a number of the electrocardiogram tracings 'were definitely abnormal, and strongly suggestive of myocarditis.' Most of the cardiologists consulted said that they would not allow swimmers or any sportsman to train *at all* if they obtained such tracings.

In view of our previous observations with various swimmers and cyclists we have proposed a theory in an earlier study[1] that the changes in the electrocardiograms are due to a general biochemical upset in the organism brought about by failure of the body to adjust fully to the extreme stress of heavy training. The results of the tests with the Australian swimmers in Townsville seemed to confirm this theory. Certainly there seems to be no evidence of *permanent* damage to the heart or the organism in general.

The salient features of this present study are that despite the very abnormal tracings the swimmers all quickly recovered with rest.

Regarding the preparation of an athlete for his peak performance, in our present state of knowledge it is difficult to apply with certainty the information we have.

The pertinent problem facing the coach and medical adviser is, *knowing* the electrocardiogram to be grossly affected, to what extent should the individual be forced to drive himself with hard training?

The affected swimmers in the Townsville study were *forced* to train just about as hard as they could, with continued poor training times and subjective distress. Eventually with lighter training all swam well. The problem briefly stated is, would these individuals have done better if they had been 'eased up,' and trained very lightly, until their electrocardiograms became more or less normal, and *then* continued with heavier training?

It should be pointed out that it has been our experience that sportsmen with distorted T waves and not feeling well, very often protect themselves either by refusing to be driven hard or by taking time off training with real or imagined minor complaints.

We suspect that many experienced swimmers have a 'built-in' safety-valve mechanism which tells them when to ease their training, protecting themselves from too much stress and consequent strain.

The Olympic-standard swimmers in this study were clearly a highly selected group who have been 'through the mill' and survived intense training in the past. They were swimmers who had proved their capability of absorbing very hard training without breakdown. With average individuals ambitious to succeed, perhaps one should be *more* careful when T wave changes appear.

We are faced with a dilemma. To reach international standard today, a swimmer must be able to absorb from three to eight miles training a day. This severe training stimulates physiological adaptation, but may cause strain and breakdown.

How far should the process of breakdown (indicated by distorted electrocardiograms and other physiological changes) be allowed to proceed before training is eased? As yet we do not have enough observations and exact knowledge to answer this question with any great degree of certainty. Training, like teaching technique, remains partly art and partly science. The aim of research is to increase the scientific knowledge that can be applied to the problem of training the individual, helping him to reach a peak performance.

REFERENCE

1. Forbes Carlile, M.Sc. and Ursula Carlile, Dip.Phys.Ed., *Australian Journal of Physical Education*, November/December 1959.
   'T Wave Changes in the Electrocardiogram Associated with Prolonged Periods of Strenuous Exercise in Sportsmen with Special Reference to Applications in Training Swimmers.'

CHAPTER TEN

Counting Heart Rates

WE have found it useful to count heart rates after 'effort' swims made at the race distances.

At the beginning of the morning training session I usually ask swimmers for an easy effort (about 80% of all-out speed) and then, after a two- or three-minute rest, a 90% effort.

If the swimmer is in poor swimming condition (which may be due to over-training) we can quickly learn this from 'below-line' performances when a relatively slow time is accompanied by a high heart rate.

At the World Congress of Physical Education in December 1956 in Melbourne I presented a scientific paper which was a preliminary report on the use of post-exercise heart rates in the prediction of maximum performance and in assessing the progress of swimmers. After this Congress we have been able to obtain more data from swimmers, which, while generally confirming the usefulness and practical nature of our approach, has also resulted in a slight modification in our method of counting.

The basic concept is that the heart-rate response during recovery from a sustained physical effort reflects the physiological cost caused by the effort. The greater the physiological cost to the body, the faster is the heart rate and the slower its return to normal. This heart-rate response can be gauged by counting the pulse at intervals after finishing. While a count over a long period gives the most accurate estimate of the heart response, the practical consideration of time (both the swimmer's and the coach's) must be considered. A minute after finishing a swim is about the limit that a swimmer should be required to wait around for making a heart-rate count.

The object of a series of experiments made in 1956 on members of the Olympic Swimming Squad training at Townsville, was to determine the closeness of the graphed relationship between the time recorded for a distance, and the heart-rate counts made for *four* minutes after finishing. I reported that for a particular stage of training (within a week or so) a good linear relationship was found for most swimmers between time for the swim and the sum of two 10-second counts, one count made directly after finishing and the other made one minute after finishing.

More recently we have used *three* 10-second counts, one started within about five seconds of finishing the swim, the second a half-minute after finishing and the third taken one minute after finishing. The *sum* of the three counts is then plotted against the time recorded for that particular swim. The time swum for a set distance (110, 220 or 440 yards usually) is represented on the vertical axis and the sum of the three heart counts on the horizontal axis of the graph. An example of such a graph made for former breast-stroke world record-holder Terry Gathercole is shown in Figure 9.

Clearly a perfect correlation between the times recorded and the sum of the three heart-rate counts for various swims would result in a *straight line* when the points were joined, but there are numerous factors which can upset such a perfect relationship. However, within a relatively short period of training (a week or two) we have found that the data from most swimmers, when graphed, lies remarkably close to a 'line of best fit' drawn through the points. When three counts were made instead of the two the correlation was better, indicating that the latter is the better procedure. For this reason the *three-count* method has now been adopted by us as standard practice. We still only require a period of one minute after the completion of the swim for counting heart rates.

Practical Considerations

Errors in counting heart rates are common, particularly when rates as high as about 200 per minute occur after a hard effort. For this reason it is important that a coach or swimmer should at first practice counting, checked by an experienced counter. When the coach is sure *he* can count accurately, he should check his pupil's own counting after effort swims.

Counting Heart Rates

We have found that swimmers, even young ones of 12 years of age, can when it is explained to them understand the signifi-

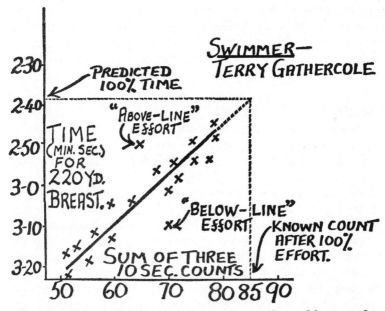

Fig. 9—Graph showing relationship between swimming time and heart rate for Terry Gathercole made during his training for the Rome Olympic Games in 1960. About three weeks after this graph was made Terry set a World Record for the 200 m and 220 yards breast-stroke with 2m 36.5 sec., about one second better than his predicted best time.

cance of the heart-rate counts. With practice and preliminary checking by means of dual counting (swimmer and coach) young swimmers soon become reliable counters. Then, after efforts, swimmers can record their times and their 10-second heart-rate counts in the coach's 'Effort Book,' and the graph from this data can be drawn later. It is sometimes easier and quicker to have a graph book at the pool-side and plot in the points of effort swims directly after the heart-rate count has been made.

In order to obtain a wide enough spread of points for drawing on the graph of the line of best fit, it is necessary for the effort swims to be widely varied (between about 80% and sometimes up to 95% of all-out speed for the distance). If all the swims are made at about the same effort, the points become clustered and the line cannot be drawn in accurately.

Over the space of a couple of weeks a swimmer's general

swimming condition usually does not vary much, thus points can be plotted on the graph from a number of effort swims made during the period to provide enough to draw a graph line. This line of best fit is drawn straight, having about as many points above as below it.

Practical Use of the Graph

With this graph as a basis for judgement, it is possible to assess the training progress and estimate the possible all-out performance of the individual at a particular stage of training.

When, after a training effort, a point is plotted which falls well 'above the line' this means that the time for the swim is relatively fast and the sum of the heart-rate counts (the physiological cost) is relatively low. Then the performance is obviously a *good* one, and the interpretation would usually be that the swimmer is improving and is in 'good form.' Swims resulting in points which fall well below the line are interpreted as representing *poor* form and a reason should be sought and appropriate action taken. Often the prescribing of less training and more rest will be the answer.

As the swimmer's endurance and co-ordination improve, *all* the points will tend to fall above the original line drawn earlier in training. This indicates that general condition has improved, as has the potential best time for an all-out swim.

In order to appreciate the change in swimming condition due to training, we have found it useful to change the appearance of the plotted points (using circles, crosses, etc.) every two or three weeks.

Prediction of All-out Time

A fairly accurate prediction of what an all-out effort would be can often be made by continuing the line of best fit until it cuts the vertical line on the graph representing the sum of the three heart-rate counts as it would be after a maximum effort. This value is often known for a swimmer from previous experience or, if such a value has not been determined, an assumption of a value of 85 will usually be fairly close to the mark and a fairly accurate prediction of all-out performance can be made on this basis.

Pulse Trough

The term 'pulse trough' is used to describe the slowing-down and subsequent speeding-up of the heart rate within the first minute or two during recovery from exercise. As swimmers get into better training, with moderate efforts (about 80%), it is not uncommon for pulse troughs to occur so that the three 10-second heart-rate counts might be recorded thus, 20, 13, 16.

The exact physiological reason for the pulse trough is not known for certain, but our observations suggest that it can be taken as an indication of good circulatory fitness and occurs when the physiological cost of the effort is low. A pulse trough, representing relatively low effort, and a relatively fast time generally reflects good swimming condition.

In the graph (see Fig. 9) made from data taken from Terry Gathercole during Empire Games training in July 1958, you will see an illustration of what is explained above. When we continue the graph line until it cuts the vertical line through the maximum heart-count value of 85, you can see it corresponds with a maximum predicted time of about 2 minutes $38\frac{1}{2}$ seconds. In fact at the end of July, Terry Gathercole swam even faster, setting the then world record of 2 minutes 36.5 seconds for 220 yards.

It is by no means *essential* to count heart rates and use this scientific control described above in order to produce good swimmers. I know plenty of excellent coaches who have never counted a pulse beat. However, I believe that the knowledge gained from heart-rate counting after efforts is well worth the small trouble involved.

Early Morning Heart Rates

Each morning on waking, while still in bed, we ask our pupils to count their heart beats for a full minute. This *basal* count is entered up daily in the swimmer's log-book.

It is now a well-known fact that training for endurance increases the power of each individual heart contraction and *decreases* the heart rate. Professor Frank Cotton was one of the first physiologists to report on this in the scientific literature. In a paper in the *Journal of Physiology*, Professor Cotton recorded that outstanding Japanese and American swimmers of the early

1930s had basal counts as low as 36 per minute when in full training.

It is interesting that an athlete's heart rate can usually be observed to decrease gradually when in hard training but increases when out of training, or if the individual is not 100% fit. During periods of hard training, relatively high early-morning counts *for the individual* can often be indicative of some degree of strain or of a bacterial infection.

Carefully taken, these counts can be a sensitive barometer of an athlete's physiological adjustment to his training.

PART III
TECHNIQUES

Introduction

THE evolution and development of modern swimming techniques makes a fascinating story, with which many great names are associated; Johnny Weissmuller, Andrew ('Boy') Charlton, Arne Borg, Dick Cavill, Freddy Lane, Fanny Durack, Cecil Healy, Rie Mastenbroek, Dawn Fraser and many others.

There is much to be learnt from studying carefully the emergence and growth of swimming techniques, because it is a story in which 'history repeats itself.' For example, the 'latest' trend today, many of us feel, is for the leg kick to play a relatively minor part in the crawl-stroke – but you will read that just after the turn of the century, when the crawl was first introduced, Syd Cavill came forward with just this idea, after watching the swimming of South Sea Island natives. That was more than sixty years ago!

Very often it was the champion swimmer with the revolutionary style, which often seemed unorthodox and 'wrong,' who in fact, set swimmers on new lines towards better performances.

We shall see that some of the theories which were popular years ago still seem valid today, but others have since been discredited. Of course, we must keep in mind the fact that intensive training, as we know it today, was not thought possible until recent years. I have a feeling that, had they done the amount and type of training we now know to be necessary, some of the great swimmers of the past, even with their 'old-fashioned' styles, might have been very close indeed to today's champions.

Here then is the story of the development of technique for speed swimming, and finally an outline of the essence of what I teach my pupils today about techniques in the four racing styles.

CHAPTER ELEVEN

First Experiments in Style

THERE is good evidence that an *over-arm* stroke was used in antiquity by the Assyrians and Greeks, at least 800 years before the birth of Christ, and that a variety of the crawl stroke was the natural style of South Sea Island natives, North American Indians and the Kaffirs of South Africa. The over-arm stroke was lost in Europe during the Dark Ages when swimming was not popular because epidemics were a constant dread, and, perhaps with some justification, swimming was believed to help the spread of plagues.

In the sixteenth century, due to such thinkers as Martin Luther and Montaigne, swimming was revived in Europe, and an under-arm dog-paddle stroke was used. The dog-paddle stroke persisted on some parts of the Continent among the Slav peoples, but in England a primitive *breast-stroke* emerged and was used in 1837 in London at the first races held by the National Swimming Society.

In the London *Times* (April 22, 1844) there is an account of a race between two North American Indians – 'Flying Gull' and 'Tobacco' – and an Englishman Kenworthy, which gives us a good idea of contemporary beliefs about technique in speed swimming. The race was over one lap of the pool, 43 yards, and of the Indians it was reported that

'Their style of swimming is totally *un-European*. They lash the water violently with their arms like the sails of a windmill and beat downward with their feet with force.'

Because the breast-stroker Kenworthy 'with the greatest ease' beat the over-arm swimmers, little notice was taken of what appeared to be the 'freak' over-arm swimming of the Indians.

English Side-stroke

During the 1840s, in a quest for greater speed, the horizontal breast-stroke gave way to a style swum on the side. In the *side-stroke* which evolved, the swimmer remained on his side throughout the stroke. Both knees were drawn up, then the legs were opened wide and swept together in a scissoring movement. From above, a side-stroker looked very like a man running. The arms were pulled back alternately so that the dead point of propulsion in the breast-stroke was to some extent overcome. Both arms were brought forward again *under* the water. This English side-stroke became the most popular racing style.

Single-arm-over Side-stroke

In 1855 in London C. W. Wallis demonstrated a new stroke to 'Professor' Fred Beckwith. Wallis came from Australia where he had seen the dark-skinned aborigines gliding through the water in the Lane Cove River at Fig Tree near Sydney. The natives brought one arm forward *over* the water.

Using the new single-arm-over side-stroke Beckwith became champion of England in 1859, and his pupil, Gardener, with a similar single-arm-over recovery triumphed in 1860. *For the next forty-six years the long-distance championship of England was won by side-strokers using the single-arm-over recovery.*

John Trudgen's Stroke

On August 11, 1873, at the Lambeth Baths, London, an Englishman, John Trudgen, made swimming history by bringing both arms over the water and winning a 160 yards handicap. The stroke he used made him the speediest sprinter of his time. Keeping flat on his chest with his head carried high in the air, Trudgen startled onlookers by swinging each arm alternately over the water and making one horizontal *breast-stroke kick* to each cycle of the arms, so that his body lifted and progressed in jerky leaps. Trudgen said he had learned his stroke from the South African Kaffirs. He had lived abroad with his father who was an engineer.

Trudgen's stroke was successful for short races, but distance swimmers like the English amateur champions Tyers and Jarvis and the Professional champion Nuttall, all wonders of the swimming world in the 1890s, *remained* single-arm-over side-strokers.

Tyers in 1895 held the English amateur record for the 220 yards with 2 minutes 41 seconds and Nuttall the professional record with 2 minutes 37 seconds.

During the 1890s swimmers started using an important modification of the single-arm-over side-stroke technique. This was written of Tyers at the time:

> 'Instead of drawing both knees well up, he has a peculiar kick, he appears to open his legs wide *with little or no drawing-up of the knees*, and then brings his legs together exceedingly fast. Of course this snap together is what all good side-strokers do, but the opening-out peculiarity is a noticeable feature of all Manchester swimmers.'

This so-called Lancashire or North of England leg kick was timed to be made when the pulling arm was practically at right angles to the shoulder under the water. Jarvis, also from the North of England, was described as being:

> 'like an electric launch going through the water, hardly a ripple, no jerk. His legs cross for the world like a pair of scissors half open.'

It was interesting to read a description of Jarvis, who later won at the Olympic Games. He was –

> 'fat all over, which literally hangs in some parts. His breasts fall like a woman's, but he has powerful shoulders and tremendous thighs.'

Modern champions are not built like this!

Double-Over-arm

During the 1890s, while most swimmers were using their own variations of the single-arm-over side-stroke, *some* were using a stroke which evolved from the one Trudgen had demonstrated. The swimmer moved from the flat position to his side and back again during each over-arm cycle. The side-stroke scissor kick replaced the breast-stroke kick of Trudgen. This stroke with the side-stroke scissor became known as the *double-over-arm*, but in England was used only for short distances and for a long time was *not* successful as a racing stroke.

Later *any* double-over-arm stroke with a side-stroke leg action

Ilsa Konrads and Lorraine Crapp, two great Australian champions. Ilsa, in January 1960, broke Lorraine's 400 metres World Record of 4 minutes 47.2 seconds with 4 minutes 45.4 seconds. At the beginning of 1963, Ilsa's time still stood as the 440 yards World Record. Lorraine Crapp made 'history' when she became the first woman to break the 5 minutes barrier for 400 metres. She did this officially at Townsville (Australia) on August 25, 1956, whilst preparing for the Olympic 400 metres which she won easily in Melbourne.

Stills from our 16 mm underwater movie film.

(*Top left*) Butterflyer Neville Hayes, from underwater. Here the bent arm pull is nearly completed, the hands practically touch as the rotating action of the forearms is completed. The breath is being taken at this late stage of the arm stroke.

(*Top right*) Neville Hayes. Here the former world record holder stretches well out and the hands enter wide of the shoulders. The first leg kick is being made at this stage, and the next will be made as the arms finish their pull.

(*Bottom left*) Terry Gathercole, world record holder in 1960 at breast-stroke. Terry's buttocks are high, maintaining the horizontal position in the water, and the leg kick is 'narrow.' In the classical breast-stroke kick, the legs would have been spread wide – causing more resistance. Terry's feet are turned out momentarily, but soon they will take up a backwards pointing, streamlined position. He has great flexibility in his ankle joints.

(*Bottom right*) Terry Gathercole, from above water. Here Terry is making the important stretch forwards at the beginning of the stroke. Notice the 'head down' position, with the chin held forward.

became known as the 'trudgen' (often misspelt trudgeon) although John Trudgen himself as we have said, actually used a *breast-stroke* kick and bounced along with shoulders horizontal whilst he recovered each arm alternately over the water.

Progress in Australia

Although there is evidence that from the time the First Fleet arrived in 1788 a good deal of swimming went on around Sydney Cove, the first regular championships in Australia were held during 1889 at the now demolished Sydney Natatorium baths in Upper Pitt Street near the Central Railway Station. Salt water was pumped from the harbour nearly two miles away.

Charlie Hellings won the first New South Wales 100 *yards* Championship in 71 seconds, but the outstanding swimmer of this period in Australia was burly W. J. 'Paddy' Gormly who came close to world record times in New South Wales Championships between 1890 and 1895. His leg action was unusual; he accompanied his single-arm-over side-stroke with a scissor kick in which 'he lifted his upper leg (his left) clean out of the water from knee to foot before thrashing it down.'

In 1892 Dr A. T. Kenny, a Melbourne man, travelled to America and competed in the National Titles where he won the 100 yards and the one mile. It was not until after 1900 that the American swimmers could match the English or Australians.

In January 1896 Percy, one of the famous Cavill family, burst on to the Australian swimming scene. Percy Cavill, a left-arm-over side-stroker, won the Australian mile championship at Windsor (N.S.W.) in the open waters of the Hawkesbury River. In this race his brother Arthur (Tums) Cavill, who was the 440 yards champion of Australia, had himself suspended by the officials, when, in an attempt to help his brother, he joined in the race for the last 200 yards fouling and injuring Gormly. These days early in the history of Australian swimming were indeed colourful! Tums, following his disqualification, became a professional and later made important contributions to speed swimming.

Success with the Double-over-arm

Around the many bays of Sydney Harbour before the turn of the century, a few youngsters were practising the *double*-over-arm. Both arms recovered over the water and the legs made the

E

side-stroke scissor kick. One of the these boys was *Freddy Lane* (who, when over 80, in 1963, was still telling stories of the early days of swimming). Another was Peter Murphy, who, on January 19, 1896, swam in the Australasian 880 yards championship, in the Cockatoo Dock, Sydney. Although Murphy was beaten by Percy Cavill and, in fact, came only third, his swim was at the time remarkable because he used the double-over-arm technique with both arms recovering out of the water for the *whole distance*. It was, according to the press:

> 'A fact perhaps without parallel in any Championship contested in the world. This particular mode of progression is so severe an attack on endurance that swimmers rarely use it over a distance exceeding 200 yards. There is no record of any other swimmer having done what Murphy did in the half-mile . . .'

In January 1899, the 18-year-old elf-like Freddy Lane performed the unprecedented feat of swimming with two arms over the water for the complete distance and winning the N.S.W. Mile Championship. It was at Wagga Wagga on the Murrumbidgee River in New South Wales.

When I saw Lane swim first in 1945 and then in 1960 the characteristics of his vigorous stroke were still evident. Lane's head was carried high and his kick was a narrowed scissor kick with a straight top leg and a narrow circling action of the underneath leg. His top leg moved sideways only about fifteen inches and its narrow whip-like closing sweep gave him considerable power in the leg drive. Swimming on his left side Lane synchronised the *beginning* of the pull of his leg with each scissor kick, thus differing in his timing from the English swimmers in Lancashire whose leg kick was made in the middle of arm stroke.

Late in 1899 Lane made his first voyage to England, where he dead-heated with Derbyshire, another double-over-arm swimmer, setting a new world record for 220 yards with 2 minutes 34.⅘ seconds. Then at the Paris Games in 1900 Lane won the 200 metres Freestyle event for Australia and proved to the world his mastery of the double-over-arm. However, the double-over-arm stroke was not to be so easily accepted by all; on July 11, 1900 appeared the following, written under the by-line of

Natator (W. F. Corbett Snr), an expert writer for the *Sydney Referee*:

'Even the best swimmers of the trudgen rarely use it for a race of more than 100 yards. In fact, the only man who depends upon it for any distance race is Fred Lane. That it is *harmful* to have to use this method of progression is shown by the fact that he is frequently so exhausted that he has to be assisted out of the water, sometimes bleeding freely through the nostrils from the strain. He has also been known to be quite prostrate for hours after the race. Never use the trudgen stroke except for short distances!'

It appears that those who break new ground in swimming technique have always had their critics!

To Summarise –

Competitive swimming had its origins in England, and from the beginning in 1837 the *breast-stroke* was the racing style. By the 1840s this gave way to the *side-stroke*, with the knees drawn up in the scissors leg kick.

In 1859 the championship of England was won with a *single-arm-over* side-stroke. Long-distance championships in England and at the Olympic Games were won with this technique for the next 45 years.

In 1875 John Trudgen introduced a style new to English racing in which *both* arms were recovered over the water. The body remained flat on the chest and the legs made an orthodox breast-stroke kick.

By the 1890s the *double-over-arm* had evolved. As with Trudgen's stroke both arms recovered over the water, but in the double-over-arm the swimmer was mainly on his side and the legs made a side-stroke scissor kick.

CHAPTER TWELVE

The Early Crawl-stroke

IT is now more than sixty years since the crawl-stroke was first swum in competition. Realising that many published accounts of the beginnings of the crawl had been inaccurate or incomplete, in the early 1950s I set about documenting the history of the crawl as a competitive stroke. At that time I was able to contact personally several of the people actually involved and also the close relatives of others. I searched through yellowing newspapers, old magazines and early swimming books. Space here does not allow me to do more than give a bare outline of a story that is full of colourful characters and sometimes bitter rivalries, as men strove for supremacy in speed swimming and the 'Australian' crawl-stroke was emerging.

One of the people to whom I spoke was Fredda Cavill. She told me some details of her father and six famous brothers, and of the early days of swimming in Australia. In August 1877 an adventurous Englishman, Fred Cavill, following the example set by Matthew Webb in 1875, determined to become the second man to swim the English Channel. Fred Cavill would have succeeded but unfortunately, during the night after he had struggled to within 50 yards of the shore of France with a strong wind blowing up, the owner of the small boat which was accompanying him refused to continue lest the boat be smashed on the rocks. So, officially the attempt failed. Twenty years later, one of his sons, Charles, became the first man ever to swim the Golden Gate at San Francisco. The Cavill's were a vigorous, highly adventurous family.

In 1879 Fred Cavill voyaged to Australia and started a swimming baths at Lavender Bay in Sydney Harbour. 'Professor' Cavill soon had a flourishing business. Of Fred Cavill's six sons, three played an important part in the development of the crawl

as a competitive stroke. Syd Cavill wrote in the *Sydney Referee*
(July 1914) his version of the birth of the crawl-stroke:

'I claim that I am the man who discovered the crawl and
that my brother Arthur ("Tums"), who died the other day in
Seattle when he froze trying to swim the harbour there, was
the first man to swim the stroke in Australia, and that my
brother Dick was the man who perfected it. I introduced it
into the United States. In 1898 I made up my mind to leave
Sydney and try my luck in America. On the way, in Apia
(Samoa) I swam against a woman and she gave me the
hardest race of my life.

'Later I watched her intently. She swam a natural crawl
stroke, *not kicking her legs at all*. I wrote home from Apia
telling Tums all about it, how I could swim with my legs tied,
using the crawl-stroke, as fast as with my legs free using any
other stroke. Tums set to work and found he could do the
same.'

To draw attention to the new crawl-stroke, so different from
the popular side-stroke, Tums challenged Sid Davis to an
unusual race. The *Referee*, November 13, 1898, describes the
historic race:

'There was a very large crowd at Davis' floating baths at
Balmain on Thursday evening, attracted by the fact that a
novel contest had been arranged to take place between Sid
Davis and Tums Cavill, the latter undertaking to swim with
his legs tied while Davis had all his limbs free. A bet of £5
hinged on the race. The course was one lap of the basin, 33
yards. Cavill led throughout and eventually won by one yard,
amid a great deal of excitement. The time was 20 seconds.'

The race, to many who saw it, proved that the leg action in
the double-over-arm stroke should be reduced and kept very
narrow. Fred Lane, one of the spectators, has since told me that
when Tums swam his ordinary stroke he employed an exag-
gerated drawing up of the top leg which other swimmers had
long recognised as a faulty, retarding action. Swimming with his
legs tied prevented this retarding action.

In 1898 a boy from the British Solomon Islands arrived in
Sydney – Alick Wickham – whose brother Harry wrote me

several letters in 1950 when I was investigating the beginnings of the crawl-stroke. These letters explained that Alick came to Australia on his father's trading schooner, when he was seven years old, and stayed in Sydney for his schooling. Alick was keen on swimming, he played around in the water continually, and in 1898 was entered in a 66 yards under-10 years handicap race in Australia's oldest rock pool at Bronte, near Sydney, and it was here that Alick astonished onlookers with his speed and unusual stroke. Charlie Bell, who raced against him, told me that Wickham 'swam with his head held fairly high, turning it quickly from side to side breathing with each complete stroke, his woolly head apparently not getting wet. The entry of his arms was short and towards the centre line of the body with the elbows well bent. His arm action was very fast and short. Each arm performed a symmetrical action with the head turning from side to side as if breathing on each side, but only breathing on *one* side to each stroke.'

Watching young Alick's speed and peculiar continuous movement through the water was George Farmer, one of the prominent swimming coaches of the day. The story has often been told of how Farmer excitedly exclaimed – 'Look at that kid *crawling*.' The name of the 'crawl'-stroke is said to come from his comment.

Dick Cavill

The Cavills were all notable swimmers. Ernest, Charles, Percy, Tums and Syd had all won championships by the time 15-year-old Dick, who was to be the greatest swimmer of them all, won his first New South Wales championship on December 31, 1899.

There is another version of the origin of the name 'crawl' as stemming from an occasion when with head down and arms flaying the water, Dick Cavill swam persistently into a rival (there were no lanes in those days) who came out after the race complaining that young Cavill was 'crawling all over me.' Early in his competitive career, Dick Cavill swam part *side*-stroke and part over-arm trudgen, but soon he was able to cover the whole of his races swimming trudgen. Then he experimented with the crawl-stroke and, according to his brother Syd, improved it by adding the vertical kick of the legs. Mind you, Dick did not always win with his new 'crawl' stroke. In December 1900, George Read defeated him to set a new world record for the 440 yards of 5 minutes 42 seconds. This was 7 seconds better than Nuttall's previous record.

Read was one of the greatest swimmers of his day. His interesting style was graphically described in the contemporary press –

'As Read rolls on to his right side with his double-over-arm his left leg draws up from the hip to such an extent that with his face screwed back to the left shoulder for inhalation he conveys the idea that he resembles the domestic cat comfortably coiled up on the hearth.'

Read bent his legs in the kick much more than the best English swimmers or most Australians, Lane and others adopted nearly straight legs and narrow kicks in their scissoring actions.

On March 2, 1901 the first printed reference to the 'crawl'-stroke appears in the *Sydney Arrow* newspaper.

'Cavill will set Hogan and company a lively go in Brisbane, especially when he gets fairly moving with that great *crawl* kick of his.'

Obviously by 1901, Dick Cavill was doing much more than trailing his legs behind him.

Dick Cavill and Fred Lane both went to England in 1902 where Cavill demonstrated his new stroke. *Before* this time Syd Cavill claims he had introduced the crawl to America. He wrote later –

'I returned to America in 1899 and taught the stroke to all the boys who swam at the San Francisco Olympic Club where I became supervisor of swimming. The first to make good use of it was J. Scott Leary, who was the first to use the crawl in a regular race in America. Leary was a cripple and had a withered leg. He finished third to De Halmay and Daniels in the Olympic 100 yards at St Louis. Then I taught the stroke to Harry Handy. He won a mile race, and did not kick his legs one inch during the whole race. The stroke did not get to the East Coast of America until much later.'

In July 1902 at Manchester, England, Fred Lane narrowly defeated Cavill and the great English swimmer Bob Derbyshire, and became the first man to swim 100 yards in 60 seconds. Two weeks later, Cavill swam 58.⅘ seconds, swimming from scratch in a handicap race. However, the honour of being the first *officially* to break the minute for 100 yards goes to Fred Lane, with 59.⅗ seconds at Leicester on October 9, 1902.

Back in Australia, Annette Kellerman, later to become a famous water-woman, established a world record of 82 seconds for the 100 yards using the double-over-arm (with the scissor kick). This was during the first series of Ladies Swimming Championships held in Australia. The year was 1902.

When he returned to Australia, Lane retired, unbeaten by Cavill, who went on in 1903 to win *all* the Australian Championships from 100 yards to the mile.

Cavill's stroke had greatly impressed English swimmers, an English newspaper report quoted in the *Sydney Referee* said –

'Cavill's marvellous crawl-stroke called forth the admiration of everybody present. His head is low in the water and he breathes by snatches, every five breaths or so. His arms extend wide and sweep under the chest.'

A more vivid account of Cavill's stroke in England was given by McArthur Moseley of Leeds, the President of the National Amateur Swimming Association. He said –

'Generally known by the appropriate name of 'Splash Cavill,' when he is swimming, you see a lot of splash and little of Cavill. One might be pardoned for mistaking him for a screw propellor that received a galvonic shock but the rate he struggles through the water is little short of a miracle. He uses a sort of revised double-over-arm of the trudgen variety. To describe it scientifically or even minutely is impossible.'

Dick Cavill must have appeared a very vigorous swimmer when he demonstrated the crawl-stroke to the English – but how *did* Cavill use his legs?

Were Wickham and Cavill 2-beaters?

What became known as the Australian Crawl-stroke was comprised of two heavy leg kicks – downward thrashes made

At fifteen years of age Dutch-born Marguerithe Ruygrok who now lives in Australia has a very streamlined body build. In 1963 Marguerithe after adopting a Jastremski-like breast-stroke technique completed the season with the excellent times for a junior swimmer of 1 minute 21.4 seconds for the 110 yards and 2 minutes 54.2 seconds for the 220 yards. Her 220 yards medley time of 2 minutes 39.6 seconds was in world class too. She swims with the Ryde Club in Sydney. In December 1964 Marguerithe swam in a course 1½ inches short of 220 yards and recorded 2 minutes 49.8 seconds. This time is now recognised as the Australian 200 metres record.

'Chet' Jastremski of Indiana University who established the World Record of 2 minutes 29.6 seconds in 1961 and was the first swimmer to better 2 minutes 30 seconds for the 200 metres breaststroke. He revolutionised the stroke by demonstrating the importance of a strong arm pull. Here his head has just 'popped up' for a breath towards the end of the arm pull just as the forearms start their final rotating action.

with the knees bent and timed so that the left leg beat synchronised with the start of the right arm pull and right arm with left
leg.

We shall see later that Cecil Healy did a great deal to
popularise the 2-beat crawl and it is usually assumed that Cavill
and Wickham swam this way.

Because we have no movie films of the pioneers when they
raced more than sixty years ago, we must rely for descriptions
on the recollections of people who saw them swim and what was
written about them at the time.

There are two schools of thought on the question, those who
claim that Wickham and Cavill were two-beaters and those who
are equally sure that they were either four- or six-beaters.

Charlie Bell, veteran Sydney swimmer and one of the pioneers
of surfing in Australia, has been closely associated with swimming since 1900, and he told me he has vivid recollections of
Dick Cavill as a two-beater who lifted his right foot well out of
the water, smashing it down so strongly that it used to splash
spectators in the gallery at the Coogee Aquarium Pool.

From the letter that follows it can be seen that Bill Hill,
secretary of the N.S.W. Amateur Swimming Association in its
early days agreed closely with Charlie Bell, that Cavill and
Wickham were two-beaters, at any rate towards the end of their
swimming careers.

Sydney,
February 2, 1954.

Dear Forbes,

I am pleased to give you my recollection of the strokes used
by Dick Cavill and Alick Wickham. It is a long time ago but
here it is. The crawl-stroke used by Dick Cavill, *in the early
period of the crawl era had very little, if any, leg work in it.* He
buried his head, and only inhaled and exhaled at long intervals.
The body moved very slightly, but the arms worked rapidly and
the legs simply trailed without movement. It must be remem-
bered that all the contests in Sydney at this time were held in
salt water with excellent floatation. The buried head also helped
to keep the legs in a good position of floatation. However, this
method, limited the the distance of the stroke's usefulness.
Initially 50 yards was the limit, as efforts to extend the distance

were made the breathing became more regular, and a slight roll of the shoulders occurred.

Swimming in fresh water in other states of Australia and in England, led to more action of the legs, as the slight roll of the shoulders to the left occurred, it gave the arm pull greater length and it was found that the beat of the right foot and leg helped to roll the body back and resume the balance ready for the slight roll of the right side and beat from the left foot and so on.

For the two or three years before his retirement Dick Cavill used the two-beat crawl. He only used it for distances to 100 yards. In longer races he swam trudgen but when outpaced, as he was on occasions by George Read and Barney Kieren in distance races, he would break into a crawl for a time and then back into the trudgen again.

Alick Wickham, as I remember him, used a slight roll and two beats with the higher head action and more regular breathing. He used up his strength quickly and rarely swam 100 yards without fading at the finishing stages.

Trusting the above may be of some use to you,

Yours sincerely,

W. W. HILL

There are many students of swimming who have backed up the two-beat version, including Fanny Durack and Bill Longworth, great two-beat swimmers of the outstanding 1912 Australian Olympic team, although Longworth, when I questioned him, made a qualification, saying 'Cavill swam a two-beat with possibly two flutters added.' Jack Dexter, another keen observer and later for twenty years chairman of the N.S.W. Amateur Swimming Association, supported the two-beat claim. So did Professor Frank Cotton, a N.S.W. champion in 1920 who, before he died in 1955, told me that he had seen Alick Wickham perform many times and had no doubt he used the two-beat timing.

But now the other side of the picture. There was hardly a more astute student of swimming than Frank Beaurepaire who had a great influence on world swimming. Before his death in 1956 he wrote in a letter to me – 'Alick Wickham was a true *six-beat* crawl swimmer. He had a perfect style and was terrific upwards of 75 yards.'

Harold Hardwick, another great swimmer and observer and a team-mate of Longworth and Fanny Durack at the 1912 Olympics, has always regarded both Cavill and Wickham as *four*-beaters. In November 1939 Hardwick wrote a significant article in which he claimed that the early Australian type of crawl was *not* confined to the two-beat, but that 'an independent leg action was first swum in competition *not* by Americans but by Cavill and Wickham. Cavill's stroke was a four-beat, but an uneven one, his right foot being lifted from the water and then thrashed down.'

Hardwick told me that in 1903, Phil Boardman of the Sydney Enterprise Club developed a natural six-beat and used it throughout his racing career. Hardwick claimed that Wickham first swam with an 'independent six-beat action' but *later* came under the influence of Cecil Healy and did a two-beat as well. There were others who have strongly argued that Wickham and Cavill used *more* than a two-beat rhythm.

Wickham's mentor, Fred Gillis, who looked after young Alick when he first arrived from the South Sea Islands, told me that he 'never counted Alick's leg beats, *but they were very fast.*' Les Bond, who knew Wickham well, and raced against him, was certain that Alick swam with 'at least a four-beat.' Club official Arthur Freeman who often saw the young Wickham at Bronte told me 'It was a six-beat which reminded me of an outboard motor.'

Sam Smith, a champion swimmer of the period was certain that – 'Cavill, like Wickham, swam with *continuous* kicks.' Sam Smith made the significant statement to me that 'the Australian two-beat crawl *started* with Cecil Healy' (that is *after* 1905).

Cecil Healy was a great performer and teacher of swimming. He was a prolific writer and before he was killed in France a few days before the end of World War I, he wrote that 'Cavill's stroke was 'a crude arrangement consisting largely of splash. It was unattractive in every way.'

Frank Beaurepaire backed up this viewpoint of lack of form of the Cavill kick in an article written in 1915 when he said that 'the Healy stroke was distinguished from the Cavill splash stroke by rhythmic movements of arms and legs.'

Cecil Healy both swam and preached 'law and order' in the leg kick. I am inclined to believe it was Healy – and *not* Cavill *or* Wickham – who first swam the Australian crawl with the well-defined two leg beats to each cycle of the arms. In 1905 he regarded the trailing, independent action of the legs an old-fashioned method.

From time to time in the history of swimming the independent leg action has been treated as something decadent. Man has always liked to systematise things, and it took Australia a long time to break away first from Healy's rigid system of the two-beat, and then many years later from the idea that the six-beat timing of the leg-kick was the last word in crawl technique.

To Summarise –

Arthur (Turns) Cavill with his legs tied, in November 1898 defeated Sid Davis, a double-over-arm swimmer who drew his knees up in his leg-kick. Cavill's success in this match race was generally interpreted as a triumph for the *straight leg* principle.

Dark-skinned Solomon Islander Alick Wickham, at the end of 1898 in the Bronte rock pool, Sydney, demonstrated what was soon to be called the *crawl-stroke*. Wickham kicked his legs in a vertical plane and was very fast for a short distance.

Dick Cavill probably acting on his brother Sid's advice, abandoned the knee-drawn-up leg action of the double-over-arm and modelled his style on that of Alick Wickham, whom he is known to have studied carefully. Dick Cavill introduced the crawl-stroke to England in the summer of 1902 but was defeated by fellow Australian Fred Lane who swam the double-over-arm with a narrow leg action and straight knees.

It is agreed by all observers of the time that the leg actions of Wickham and Cavill were vigorous vertical thrashes. There is *no general agreement* as to whether these two pioneers used two, four or more leg-beats to one revolution of the arms.

Cecil Healy of Australia was the disciple of the heavy *2-beat* leg-kick which became known as the *Australian Crawl* and was used by Healy himself and such champions as Fanny Durack and Bill Longworth.

CHAPTER THIRTEEN

Experiments with the Crawl

THE improvement in the times of winners at Olympic Games represent to some extent the results of experiments in technique, and serve as land-marks in the progress of swimming.

We shall base our story about changing ideas of technique on these results.

OLYMPIC WINNERS, MEN'S FREESTYLE

100 *Metres*

1896	Athens	Hajos	Hungary	1 min. 22.2 sec.
1900	Paris	Lane	Australia	2 min. 25.2 sec.
			(for 200 m – there was no 100 m event)	
1904	St Louis	DeHalmay	Hungary	1 min. 2.8 sec.
			(for 100 yd)	
1908	London	Daniels	U.S.A.	1 min. 5.6 sec.
1912	Stockholm	Kahanamoku	U.S.A.	1 min. 3.4 sec.
World War I				
1920	Antwerp	Kahanamoku	U.S.A.	60.4 sec.
1924	Paris	Weissmuller	U.S.A.	59.0 sec.
1928	Amsterdam	Weissmuller	U.S.A.	58.6 sec.
1932	Los Angeles	Miyazaki	Japan	58.2 sec.
1936	Berlin	Csik	Hungary	57.6 sec.
World War II				
1948	London	Ris	U.S.A.	57.3 sec.
1952	Helsinki	Scholes	U.S.A.	57.4 sec.
1956	Melbourne	Henricks	Australia	55.4 sec.
1960	Rome	Devitt	Australia	55.2 sec.

400 *Metres*

1896	Athens	Neumann	Austria	8 min. 12.6 sec.
				(for 500 m)
1900	Paris	Jarvis	Great Britain	13 min. 40.2 sec.
				(for 1,000 m)

400 *Metres*

1904	St Louis	Daniels	U.S.A.	6 min. 16.2 sec. (for 440 yd)
1908	London	Taylor	Great Britain	5 min. 36.8 sec.
1912	Stockholm	Hodgson	Canada	5 min. 24.4 sec.
World War I				
1920	Antwerp	Ross	U.S.A.	5 min. 26.8 sec.
1924	Paris	Weissmuller	U.S.A.	5 min. 4.2 sec.
1928	Amsterdam	Zorilla	Argentina	5 min. 1.6 sec.
1932	Los Angeles	Crabbe	U.S.A.	4 min. 48.4 sec.
1936	Berlin	Medica	U.S.A.	4 min. 44.5 sec.
World War II				
1948	London	Smith	U.S.A.	4 min. 41.0 sec.
1952	Helsinki	Boiteux	France	4 min. 30.7 sec.
1956	Melbourne	Rose	Australia	4 min. 27.3 sec.
1960	Rome	Rose	Australia	4 min. 18.3 sec.

1,500 *Metres*

1896	Athens	Hajos	Hungary	18 min. 22.2 sec. (for 1,200 m)
1900	Paris	Jarvis	Great Britain	58 min. 24 sec. (for 4,000 m)
1904	St Louis	Rausch	Germany	27 min. 18.2 sec. (for 1,760 yd)
1908	London	Taylor	Great Britain	22 min. 48.4 sec.
1912	Stockholm	Hodgson	Canada	22 min. 0 sec.
World War I				
1920	Antwerp	Ross	U.S.A.	22 min. 23.2 sec.
1924	Paris	Charlton	Australia	20 min. 6.6 sec.
1928	Amsterdam	Borg	Sweden	19 min. 51.8 sec.
1932	Los Angeles	Kitamura	Japan	19 min. 12.4 sec.
1936	Berlin	Terada	Japan	19 min. 13.7 sec.
World War II				
1948	London	McLane	U.S.A.	19 min. 18.5 sec.
1952	Helsinki	Konno	U.S.A.	18 min. 30.3 sec.
1956	Melbourne	Rose	Australia	17 min. 58.9 sec.
1960	Rome	Konrads	Australia	17 min. 19.6 sec.

For the first Modern Olympic Games in Athens (1896) the winners in all the swimming events used the single-arm-over side-stroke, but by the Paris Games in 1900 the double over-arm was established as the fastest stroke for sprint events. Fred Lane (Australia) won the 200 m sprint (there was no 100 m) in the River Seine. He swam with his head held high, and used one narrow scissor kick to each revolution of the arms. England's burly John Jarvis side-stroked, with one arm recovering over the water, to win both the 1,000 m and 4,000 m free-style events.

Lane once told me of the leg action of Zoltan de Halmay (Hungary), who swam second to him in the 1900 Games. With his legs trailing behind him and using a double over-arm stroke, de Halmay was virtually swimming the crawl – at that time being developed in Australia. De Halmay won the 100 yards Olympic event at St Louis in 1904, and finished his career by swimming a close second to Daniels four years later.

In the early years of the century, the principle of the crawl-stroke spread from Australia to America. At San Francisco, Syd Cavill was teaching the crawl-stroke at the Olympic Club, where some Americans were using it successfully.

On the East Coast of America, Louis de B. Handley was experimenting. He has given this account –

'In 1903 I received from Australia newspaper clippings describing the Australian crawl in which the left leg beat was synchronised with the right arm stroke. I took the clippings to the New York Athletic Club's pool, and with other club-mates tried unsuccessfully to get the hang of it. A few days later Gus Sundstrum, the pool manager, gave an exhibition of what he called the "Swordfish Glide," shooting down the pool with arms outstretched in front of his head, face submerged, legs almost straight and feet moving in scissoring action under the surface.

'N.Y.A.C. swimmers, thinking the leg drive was identical with the Australian crawl adopted it, and in 1904 two members, Jack Lawrence and Van Cleaf, covered 50 yards in 26 seconds, lowering the American record.'

The Americans took the Australian crawl and experimented with it. They developed an *independent* and *continuous* leg beat and using this the tall, 205-lb. Charles Daniels soon became the first great swimmer from the United States of America.

Daniels won the 440 yards event (it was yards not metres) at the St Louis Games in 1904. In 1907 Daniels wrote a book, *Speed Swimming*, and in advance of his time he came close to modern ideas on the crawl. Comparing the Australian stroke with the American he wrote –

'In America with few exceptions the arms and legs are worked independently and the thrash has a narrower scope, the legs being opened less.

'In the American crawl the continuous action of the legs keeps the body constantly in motion.

'The relative timing of the arms and legs in the American crawl can best be determined by the individual or his coach, one with strong arms and weak legs can adopt a rapid arm motion and a slow kick, one with strong legs can do the opposite.

'This is one of the stroke's best features for it can be fitted to each person. Some of our best men use the arms almost entirely, and one at least, Mr H. J. Handy of Chicago, lets his legs trail behind him. He tried the kick but found he could not swim without tiring when using it, so he abandoned it. Others can go almost as fast with legs alone as when using the arms and legs.'

Daniels, with his independent but fairly rigid leg action, won the 100 m Olympic event in 1908, and in 1910 made a new world record for the 100 m by swimming 62.8 seconds. This was in a 25 m course, in which world records were allowed until 1956.

Although the crawl was established as the fastest stroke for short races (100 m and less), the best *distance* swimmers still used the trudgen style.

One of the first great trudgen swimmers, whose performances provided 'proof' to many that the crawl-stroke was only good for sprints, was the Australian, Bernard Bene ('Barney') Kieren, who burst into prominence in 1904 virtually forcing Dick Cavill into retirement. Within a year he had captured every world record from 220 yards to the mile. Kieren's remarkable record for the mile of 23 minutes 16.⅘ seconds made in the 50-yard course of Sydney's Lavender Bay Baths was unbeaten for sixteen years until in 1921 Olympic winner Norman Ross of U.S.A. recorded 22 minutes 58.4 seconds in the 33⅓-yard course at the Coogee Aquarium Baths in Sydney.

Kieren's phenomenal swims were made between January 1904 and December 1905. Then following a visit to England, where he proved master of the great Dave Billington, Kieren died after an appendix operation in Brisbane, where he was competing in the Australian Championships. He was 19.

Although he swam the double-over-arm (so-called trudgen stroke) Barney Kieren's best times included 5 minutes 19 seconds for the 440 yards and 11 minutes 11.6 seconds for the 880 yards. Not until fifteen years later, in the early 1920s, did swimmers anywhere in the world approach Kieren's times, but his name appears only once on the list of world records (for the 500 yards swum in England in 1904). The International Swimming Federation (F.I.N.A.) which was constituted in 1908, in retrospect recognised only one of Kieren's records, although there is little doubt of their authenticity. Many of his times had been established from the scratch mark in handicap races.

Another great trudgen swimmer was Harry Taylor of Great Britain, who won both the 400 m and the 1,500 m Olympic events in 1908. In his stroke he drew both knees well up before sweeping the legs together, once for every arm cycle.

Australian Frank Beaurepaire, later Sir Frank and Lord Mayor of Melbourne, swam the trudgen in a competitive career extending from 1906 to 1928. He had the distinction of being placed in Olympic finals from 1908 to 1924. In 1910 he toured Europe as teacher and competitor and was undefeated. At various times he held fourteen world records.

Early in his career Beaurepaire swam with a single, wide scissor kick, but when he returned from overseas in 1910 he had introduced the vertical crawl thrash between the wide scissor kicks. His lower leg bent at the knee, which he drew up before making the trudgen sweep. In this respect his leg action differed from the *trudgen-crawl* kick, which had evolved in America parallel with the independent leg action of Daniels.

Handley has written (*Encyclopaedia Britannica* Ed. 1951) of American swimmers' development of the trudgen-crawl. He said –

'In attempting to imitate the Australian crawl action they unwittingly developed a faster leg stroke, executing four scissoring kicks per stroke. The new leg drive was combined by the Americans with the double over-arm of the trudgen and the resulting stroke was christened the four-beat crawl to distinguish it from the two-beat Australian crawl.

'Meanwhile experiments had led to the belief that the four-beat leg thrash was effective when composed of one comparatively wide and three very narrow scissoring motions. This style, termed the four-beat trudgen-crawl or four-beat single rhythm crawl became the accepted racing medium.'

In 1911 the Australian crawl with its heavy *two*-beat kick, put to the test. Had Healy sufficiently perfected the stroke for distance races to win the N.S.W. three-quarter-mile Championship? Would he defeat Frank Beaurepaire, the greatest all-round swimmer of that time, and place the seal of practicability on the crawl stroke for distance races?

The memorable race drew the biggest crowd on record to the Sydney Domain Baths and brought to light the hitherto unknown Bill Longworth. Young Longworth caused a sensation when he led all the way to win by 20 yards from the two famous swimmers Healy and Beaurepaire. Longworth used a perfect two-beat Australian crawl. The two-beat crawl-stroke had triumphed in Australia! In 1912 Longworth went on to win every Australian championship from 100 yards to the mile, a feat to date only equalled by Dick Cavill (1903), John Marshall (1949) and John Konrads (1959). In 1963 Robert Windle missed out when defeated by a fingertip by David Dickson in the 110 yards.

Healy had improved the crawl-stroke by demonstrating that regular breathing was possible. Now Longworth had.won with it from a good field in a long-distance race. It seemed then that the Australian crawl was the stroke for the future. In 1911 Cecil Healy wrote –

'The first difficulty to be conquered in the crawl was that of getting the breath without interfering with the rate of progress.

'I was the first to overcome the problem of breathing regularly. Even today, such as Daniels, de Halmay and Hardwick breathe only now and again.

'Hitherto I swam with the muscles more or less set and hard, but watching Beaurepaire's trudgen I noticed his movements were extraordinarily free and easy. I commenced to practise with my muscles relaxed.'

Healy had improved the crawl-stroke, although he still insisted on the two-beat leg kick.

1912 *Olympics*
Two Australian girls, Mina Wylie and Fanny Durack, both using the two-beat Australian crawl, led the world in 1912 at the Stockholm Olympics, when they finished first and second in the first women's event held at the Olympics – the 100 m freestyle.

In the season 1910–11 Mina Wylie had performed the unparalleled feat of winning every N.S.W. and Australian Women's Championship at freestyle, breast-stroke and back-stroke. Fanny Durack established eleven world records between 1912 and 1918.

Cecil Healy swam second to the new sprint sensation, Duke Kahanamoku of Hawaii, in the Olympic 100 m in 1912, but once again in this Olympic Games the crawl-stroke was *not* used successfully by competitors in distance events.

Using the trudgen-crawl with a slight drawing-up of one knee, George Hodgson of Canada took the 400 m and 1,500 m Olympic titles in then remarkable times which stood for twelve years as Olympic records. Trudgen-crawlers, Hatfield of England and Hardwick of Australia were second and third.

Duke Kahanamoku's win in the 100 m at Stockholm with 1 minute 3.4 seconds set the experts thinking. His leg action was the forerunner of the modern flutter kick, faster and more flexible in its action than the 'independent' kick used by Daniels.

Kahanamoku swam very high, with his shoulders clear of the water. His heels were mainly under the surface and his kick made very little splash. Healy described the kick as being

'like a propeller in action, the water boils and bubbles around the feet. The leg action is made from the hips. He does not bend the knees like we do.'

Kahanamoku advocated and used a pull well under the centre of the body with his arms bent.

Two problems were bothering the Australian swimmers and coaches after the Olympic Games of 1912. One was whether the crawl-stroke *was* the best stroke to use for *long* distances, and the other was whether the Australian two-beat stroke was as efficient as the 'independent' leg action being used in America.

Healy, the great exponent and protagonist of the two-beat had this to say –

> 'One of the results of our visit to Stockholm has been to create a craze here for dispensing with the established regulated movement of the right arm and leg simultaneously, in favour of the independent action of Kahanamoku and McGillivray. Before our departure we would advise a youth to rid himself of the habit but now Longworth is practising the independent leg action crawl.'

The visit of Duke Kahanamoku to Australia in season 1914–15 brought things to a head. In his first swim in Australia over the straight 100-yard course at the Sydney Domain, the tall well-tapered Hawaiian, using his spectacular crawl with an independent kick, swam a world record of 53.6 seconds.

However, 'the Duke' was beaten a few days later in the N.S.W. 440-yard Championship by trudgen-crawl swimmer Tommy Adrian of Manly, and Adrian's time of 5 minutes 38 seconds was not fast even for those days.

Healy stuck to his guns when he wrote in 1915 –

> 'I am still prepared to maintain that a good trudgen swimmer will always be able to demonstrate his superiority over a crawler beyond 200 m in fresh water. My prominence in swimming dates back from the time I commenced to exploit the crawl. I won my first and last championship with it. However, if I had devoted myself to the trudgen I would have made corresponding improvement. The Americans in small tanks (short pools) by means of a non-ceasing variety of kicks have put up good times, but I strongly recommend youths to emulate Barny Kieren or Frank Beaurepaire.'

However, the future trend of events was to prove that Bill Longworth's judgment on this matter was better than Healy's. It will always stand to the credit of Longworth's vision that he wrote at the time:

> 'I am certain from my own knowledge of swimming that

the crawl-stroke is the greater stroke over *any* distance even
though it is only in its babyhood.'

Beaurepaire agreed with Healy and wrote an article on the
crawl-stroke in 1915, coming out *against* the crawl being used
for distance races. However it is interesting to note that he
stressed an important principle to be revived fifty years later
when he maintained that the *'legs must dance attendance on the
arms.'*
Beaurepaire wrote:

'Very little attention should be given to the legs in the
crawl. In the Hungarian crawl very little attention is paid to
leg actions save that they wriggle about. Care must be taken
at all times not to make the arm actions secondary to the
legs. The Americans use a different principle from the
Australians. Their's is an independent and irregular action of
the legs known as the American or Independent crawl. This
will certainly *never* be used above the sprint distances, and I
fancy it will eventually be forsaken for the equally fast and
more versatile Australian two-beat crawl.'

L. de B. Handley records that the Americans had thought
along similar lines. Most coaches clung for a time to teaching
the slow tempo trudgen-crawl kick, believing – according to
Handley – that 'the swift leg thrash would prove entirely too
laborious for distances longer than 100 yards.'
Handley goes on to tell in the *Encyclopaedia Britannica* how
the swimming experimenters got to work:

'Late in 1917 two young champions of the New York
Women's Swimming Association, Miss Charlott Boyle and
Miss Clare Gilligan, determined to give the six-beat crawl a
trial and by the summer of 1918 broke records with it over the
longer regulation courses, 880 yards and a mile. So convincing was this demonstration that it caused a sudden change
in mind among coaches and competitors. The six-beat immediately won favour in the United States. Then another of its
champions, Miss Ethel McGary, successfully exploited in turn
the eight-beat and ten-beat varieties of the crawl, achieving
title and record honours.'

Using an eight-beat crawl-stroke all the way, Miss Gertrude Ederle of the U.S.A. swam the English Channel in 14 hours 34 minutes, breaking by nearly two hours the men's record for the course. This was in 1926.

In 1920, after the first world war which brought about the eight-year gap between Olympics, Kahanamoku, then thirty years old, regained his 100 m title and Norman Ross of the U.S.A. won both the 400 m and the 1,500 m titles.

Ross, 6 feet 2 inches tall and weighing $14\frac{1}{2}$ stone (203 lb.), used a stroke here described in detail by Les Duff, manager of the Australian swimming team. Duff wrote this when he returned in 1920 from the Antwerp Games.

'The Ross stroke is new to the world. The main difference is the kick. The Australian crawl is a thrash from the knee, synchronous with the opposite arm. The American crawl kick is a flutter, the leg work being quite independent of the arm action. Norman Ross has neither a flutter nor a thrash, but a series of modified scissor kicks, the legs working from the hips. There are two minor kicks delivered vertically when the body is on the face, and one major kick delivered horizontally when he rolls on the right side for a breath. Ross has a long reach and a steady pull, the arm action being slow enough to enable the two minor and one major scissor kicks.'

Ross was the first Olympic winner at the 400 m *not* to bend one of his knees in the so-called trudgen action. Although Ross did not use an 'independent' crawl kick with his long loping style, he may be said to be the first swimmer at Olympics to use the crawl-type stroke as distinct from the bent-knee trudgen and meet with success at distances beyond 100 m.

During October 1920, the year of Norman Ross's Olympic triumph, a tall, 15-year-old boy came under the notice of coach William Bachrach at the Illinois Athletic Club, Chicago. He was John Weissmuller, destined to pioneer new techniques which would soon make him the greatest swimmer of his time. He was to give speed swimming the greatest impetus since the Cavills first experimented with the crawl-stroke, twenty years before.

The Weissmuller crawl technique has had a tremendous influence on competitive swimming. It has in fact served as a model up to the present day.

During a swimming career extending from 1920 until he retired at the end of 1928, John Weissmuller broke every world freestyle record from 100 yards to 880 yards. In the days before the fast 'tumble turn' his best 100-yards time of 51 seconds, established in 1927, stood for sixteen years (until Alan Ford swam 50.6 seconds in 1943). Weissmuller's world record for the 880 yards made in the 110-yard course of the Honolulu Natatorium was 10 minutes 22.2 seconds.

In his book, *Swimming the American Crawl*, written in 1930 in collaboration with a journalist Clarence Bush, Weissmuller and his coach Bachrach set out in detail their theory of Weissmuller's stroke which he called the 'American Crawl.'

In essence, here are the principles of that stroke.

Weissmuller's body position was high. He says, 'My whole torso rides high on the surface of the water. Only my hips and legs are submerged. This position is achieved by arching the back up and getting tremendous power with the leg drive.'

Weissmuller developed what became known as the flutter kick, with loose legs, turned-in pigeon toes and flexible ankle joints. The leg movement was from the hips, with slightly bending knees. It was called a 'whiplash' action by Bachrach. The maximum depth of the kick from the heel of one foot to the toe of the other was about 18 inches.

It is very significant that, although Weissmuller developed a very effective leg drive, Bachrach believed that the kick should be subordinated to the arm action. Weissmuller made no effort after his initial learning period to kick a regular six-beat. This is what he said about timing the kick:

'When anybody tries to involve coach Bachrach in an argument as to how many leg beats should be taken with each revolution of the arms, he laughs and waves the whole argument aside. He taught me that as the arms were the main propelling force in the crawl-stroke the legs must be subordinated. There is power in the leg beat so that it is probably in this department that I gain my margin of superiority over my rivals, but this power is chiefly to maintain a high body position and it is secondary, and attention must not be concentrated on it at the expense of the arm action.'

Weissmuller says he made the discovery in Honolulu that he could swim better at the 880 yards by adopting a *two-beat flutter kick* action. As we shall see later, the principle of reducing the leg kicks for distances has been tried successfully by distance swimmers for more than thirty years, culminating in the action of Murray Rose.

Weissmuller endeavoured to keep his shoulders flat on the water so that there was very little shoulder roll in his stroke.

His arm pull was made from a point straight in front of the shoulder with his elbow bent throughout at about 45 degrees from the straight position. He concentrated on making what he called a backward pull, that is, there was very little shoulder lean into the stroke. Weissmuller made a feature of the 'push' at the end of the stroke and his hands came out of the water fairly wide at the thighs.

His arm recovery was made with a loose round-arm swing with moderately high elbows and, as in the pull, the forearm was bent at approximately 45 degrees from the straight-arm position.

Weissmuller described the timing of the stroke thus – 'The instant before the the right arm loosens hold upon leverage at the hips, my left arm starts down.' In other words the speed of the arm recovery was only very slightly faster than the catch so that there was practically *no* 'overtaking' arm action.

Unlike Kahanamoku, who snatched a breath every four strokes, Weissmuller breathed regularly and fully with each revolution of his arms. He advocated inhaling through the mouth and exhaling *gradually* through the nose whilst the head was turned toward the front.

At the Paris Olympics in 1924, Weissmuller swam the 100 m in 59 seconds, comfortably defeating Duke Kahanamoku by 2.4 seconds – the easiest win ever in an Olympic sprint. Sam Kahanamoku was 0.4 seconds behind his brother in third place.

At the same games, Weissmuller swam his (by then famous) crawl-stroke in the 400 m and won in 5 minutes 4.2 seconds, a world and Olympic record. The Swede, Arne Borg with 5 minutes 5.6 seconds and Australian Andrew 'Boy' Charlton 5 minutes 6.6 seconds, were close behind.

John Weissmuller's feat in winning both the 100 m and 400 m was the first and last time this double has been performed at the

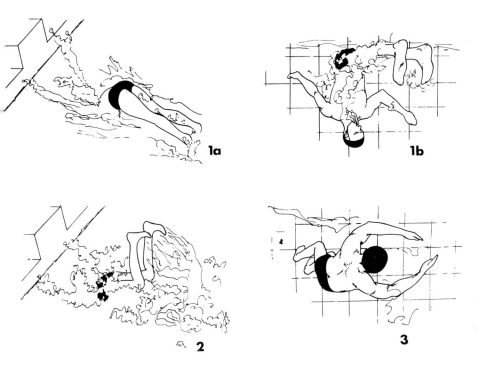

1a

1b

2

3

The Tumble Turn

Geoff Shipton was one of the fastest tumble turners Australia has had. In 1958 in a specially arranged 'match' in the Natatorium, Hawaii, Geoff repeatedly beat American Dick Cleveland who was recognised as a great turner. This is an analysis made from our 16 mm instructional film.

1a. Shipton's left arm has stretched well out and touched the wall. He is bending at the waist keeping the legs as straight as possible. The head is being pushed under the left arm as the body tumbles over.

1b. Underwater, taken at the same stage as 1a. International rules insist that the wall be touched by the hand.

2. Above water, the legs are thrown over *clear* of the water and almost thud on to the wall. During the latter part of this movement the body will twist on to its side.

3. Underwater. Now comes a very important point in the tumble, the swimmer must push off quickly with the feet in the same position as they landed on the wall A twist on to the face-down position at this stage will waste time and slow down the turn. See text on page 193.

A Racing Start

These drawings of John Devitt were made from our movie film. It is interesting that Devitt, the gold medal winner in the 100 metres sprint at Rome, once used to take up a starting position with his arms stretched well back. He was not a fast starter until team mates talked him into trying the type of start he demonstrates here, which he quickly mastered.

1. 'Take your marks': arms in a slightly forward position.

2. 'Go': the arms are immediately flung slightly forward, around and backwards as the body topples forwards, and the heels are raised.

3. Then when the legs are ready to make their powerful extension, the arms are swinging downwards and forwards. The two actions thus coincide and the 'timing' of the dive is correct.

4. John Devitt's body is rigid and straight with feet pointed. He cuts the water like a knife. First there is a glide and then the legs kick strongly to drive the body to the surface before the first arm stroke. See text on page 194.

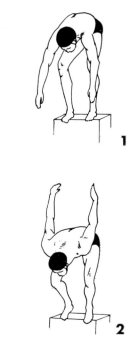

1

2

3

4

Olympic Games

At Paris Americans took all the places in the women's 100 m and the 400 m freestyle. Ethel Lackie (1 minute 12.4 seconds), who was coached by Bachrach and swam very much like Weissmuller, won the sprint and Martha Norelius won the 400 m in 6 minutes 2.2 seconds. All the American girls were six- or eight-beat crawl-strokers and were much influenced by the Weissmuller technique.

Let us now examine the styles of other great swimmers of the Weissmuller era.

In the 1,500 m Olympic race in 1924, Andrew Charlton of Australia broke the world and Olympic record when he won by nearly a lap, defeating the Swede, Arne Borg (20 minutes 41.4 seconds) and Australian Frank Beaurepaire (20 minutes 48.4 seconds).

Charlton and Borg, during the 1920s, were the two greatest distance swimmers in the world. Their techniques were a far cry from the stroke of Weissmuller.

Beaurepaire, dethroned as Australian champion by 'Boy' Charlton, wrote an interesting appreciation of his rival's style –

'Charlton was first brought to my notice as a boy of 13 by Tommy Adrian, the man who beat Kahanamoku in Sydney. To Adrian must go the credit for young Charlton's development. The negative or retarding movement in the old trudgen scissor kick was removed or eliminated and the crawl leg flutters added. Fooling and swimming around the Manly baths since babyhood in the calm delightful water has taught a boy what possibly only a score of men have learned in the past twenty years. His propulsion is continuous and ever forward.'

The tall, powerfully built Charlton swam with a leg action not unlike Norman Ross. At the time, experts called his stroke the *single trudgen-crawl*. The wide scissor kick was made horizontally at the end of the left arm drive, when the body was turned well on to the side. Then followed two or three smaller vertical crawl kicks.

Arne Borg suffered defeat by Charlton at the Paris Olympics, as he had in Australia shortly before the Games. However, Borg was to improve greatly. Up to 1924 he had not trained hard, even for those days, but stung by his defeats he applied himself well. Charlton returned to work on a sheep property in New South Wales and could only swim for a few months each summer. He never competed in an Australian Championship.

Borg was tall and slim, with thin legs. He had a large chest, and swam high in the water, with his back arched and his legs seemingly trailing like threads behind him. Borg swam with his feet in a pigeon-toed position. In order to streamline his legs and trail his feet in a pointed position he used to carry out an exercise where the body weight was supported on hands and insteps (just as we teach swimmers to do in their 'body presses' today). This trained his feet to point and cut down water resistance.

In 1924 Longworth analysed the Borg kick as being 'a narrow three-beat for long-distance races and a five-beat for sprints.' His arms moved in a fast choppy action. He did *not* finish his arm pulls with a push at the end.

The greatness of Arne Borg can be judged from the fact that in Bologna, Italy, in 1927 he cut nearly 50 seconds off Charlton's world record for the 1,500 m with a then remarkable swim of 19 minutes 17.2 seconds. This time stood for eleven years, until the Japanese Amano recorded 18 minutes 58.8 seconds in 1938. Even at the 1948 Olympic Games in London, Jim McLane's winning time in the 1,500 m was only 19 minutes 18.5 seconds.

The following story is often told to illustrate Borg's courage and determination. It was at the European Championships that he swam the 1,500 m record. Playing water-polo for Sweden in the morning had two teeth knocked out, but, nothing daunted, he made his remarkable 1,500 m time *that same afternoon*.

At the 1928 Olympics in Amsterdam there were a few changes in the overall freestyle picture. Weissmuller retained his position as the world's best sprinter, but the crawl swimmer, Zorilla of Argentina, surprised everyone by defeating both Charlton and Borg in the 400 m. Then Borg reversed the 1924 result and defeated Charlton in the 1,500 m. The Frenchman, Jean Taris and Crabbe of the U.S.A. demonstrated new techniques at Amsterdam which like Weissmuller's stroke were to have considerable influence on swimming styles.

Taris swam with a flat body position and a wide *straight-armed* recovery. His arms were thrown loosely, with hands entering thumb-first nearly on the centre line. The hands squared themselves as they pulled inwards, making an S-shaped movement under the body. The elbows bent considerably underwater and then straightened as the hands pulled out wide of the hips. The Taris stroke with its straight, scythe-like recovery of the arms was known as the 'European' stroke. It was later taken up by the Hungarians.

The Frenchman's breathing was also revolutionary. Jean Taris was the first *bi-lateral* breather. He turned his head to breathe on alternate sides so that he took two breaths to each three complete arm cycles. Taris breathed in this way when he raced, and with his bi-lateral breathing he kept very flat on the water.

Taris had a remarkably large lung capacity. When he visited Australia in 1934 his vital capacity was measured at the Sydney University and found to be 6.5 litres. The average man of his height has a capacity of approximately 4.5 litres.

As a result of his careful observation of the American Clarence Crabbe, Jean Taris later developed one of the most efficient leg actions of his time. Concentrating on the *up-beat* action of the feet, he was able to drive the kicking board 50 m in 40 seconds. He developed supple legs and very loose ankles.

The sprinter Stephan Barany of Hungary, who was second in the 100 m to Weissmuller in 1928, also swam with the straight arm recovery and a central placing of the hands for the arm pull. Barany pulled under the water with arms in a straighter position than did Taris.

Clarence Crabbe became one of the first of a line of swimmers to use a *high peaked elbow* in the recovery of the arms. With a hollowed back he had a high position in the water and used little body roll. During his arm recovery the elbow was raised very high with the forearm hanging limply as the hand swung in an outward curve before the arm was straightened forward and the hand extended in front of the head. The pull was on the centre line of the body, the elbow making its greatest underwater bend half-way through the drive. There was a long pull back. When the elbow reached the surface the forearm swept on until the arm was pointing almost straight backwards. Then the elbow was lifted vertically.

Crabbe's leg action, which showed no obvious timing with the arms, was very loose and low in the water, it had a preponderance of up-thrust. There was very little bending at the knees.

Crabbe developed his 'peaked elbows' stroke in Hawaii. The Hawaiian Kalili brothers, and then Helen Madison of Seattle (U.S.A.), who won the 100 m and 400 m for women at Los Angeles in 1932, were leading exponents of this high elbow technique.

At the 1932 Los Angeles Olympics, Crabbe touched off Taris in the 400 m, but the 100 m and 1,500 m went to *Japan* when Miyazaki won the sprint and 14-year-old Kitamura, the youngest and smallest competitor in the field, won the 1,500 m.

The Japanese leapt into the limelight at Los Angeles with the greatest team of male swimmers the world had seen. So it was to Japan that the swimming world looked for the next advances in technique. In the history of swimming, following the 1932 Los Angeles Olympics, comes the 'Japanese Era.'

CHAPTER FOURTEEN

The Japanese Era

AT the Olympic Games in 1932, Japanese men dominated the swimming events, winning five out of a possible six gold medals and gaining eleven out of a possible eighteen places. The U.S.A. took four places.

Japan first entered swimmers at the Olympics in 1920, but none advanced beyond the semi-finals. At Paris in 1924 several Japanese qualified for finals, including Takaishi (fifth in 100 m and 1,500 m) and Saiti (sixth in back-stroke). In Amsterdam four years later Takaishi moved up to third place in the 100 m, Tsuruta won the gold medal for the 200 m breast-stroke, and the Japanese 4 × 200 m team finished second. Following this, a surge of confidence and optimism swept through Japanese swimming circles. The world's best swimmers, including Weissmuller and Borg, accepted invitations to compete in Japan practically every year in the 1920s and '30s, and Japanese swimmers competed in International Meets all over the world, just as once again they have since 1960. They were making every effort to learn.

Their training was well organised and for those days severe. During a period of three months' hard training a total of four or five miles was covered each day. This was done in two training sessions. Stretching and flexibility exercises were a feature of their preparation.

Progress was rapid under the centrally organised and enthusiastic Japanese National Swimming Association. By 1932, Japan's swimmers in all strokes were nearly unbeatable. Throughout the 1930s there was a great deal of discussion about the Japanese successes. The world wanted to know *why*. Naturally their techniques came under close observation. This is what Matsuzawa, the chief Japanese coach said after the Los Angeles Games.

'The 1932 victory of the Japanese was probably due to the better use of the American crawl and European racing strokes than the Americans or Europeans themselves. Added to this, the Japanese swimmers were imbued with the national spirit and if there be any one main difference it was this fact. But for the Japanese swimmers to adopt the foreign racing style in its entirety was disadvantageous. In the crawl and back-stroke Japanese swimmers endeavoured to aid the pull of the arm-stroke by the *very strong beating* of the legs. They have flexible ankles which gives them a lot of propulsion from their kicks without much effort.'

Although it was claimed by the Japanese coach that there was nothing new about the Japanese crawl technique, certainly by 1936 a distinct stroke had emerged. The famous Japanese swimmer Katsuo Takaishi, veteran of three Olympic Games and a great student of swimming, maintained that there was a gulf of difference between the Japanese style and either the American or the European styles when he wrote in 1936 for *Ashi Sports Magazine*.

The model the Japanese had studied most was John Weissmuller, and Miyazaki the sprint winner at Los Angeles, carried his arms around in the recovery with an arm sweep characteristic of the American. However, as we shall see, this feature soon disappeared from the Japanese crawl, then developing along its own lines.

The Japanese Crawl

The arm recovery became quickened and shortened, the hand entering only a short distance in front of the shoulder, followed by a long underwater glide forwards. The arm pull was made on a line under the shoulder parallel to the backbone with the elbow slightly bent. There was a 'snap' finish to the arm drive by most Japanese, although the hands came out relatively short at the line of the hips.

Some Japanese swimmers also developed a marked 'overlapping' action of the arms, due to the very quick recovery. Both arms were clearly in the water at the same time, one finishing its drive whilst the other was pushing forwards and downwards. During the arm recovery and early arm drive a continuous, powerful leg beat drove the body forward over the leading hand. In contrast to the Americans the Japanese did not carry their heads and shoulders high in the water, although the body position was sloping, the knees were the lowest part of the body. With this stroke considerable body roll was introduced for the first time amongst modern champions. As the arms drove downwards, the shoulders in turn were allowed to follow.

The leg action was based on the low hip position. The knees were moderately bent during the kick – very distinctly a *downward* and backward thrust with the feet. The feet did not come below the level of the knees so that the kick was *relatively shallow*.

The Japanese leg action was generally a continuous, 'independent' six-beat *without accent*, like Kitamura's, the 1,500 m winner at Los Angeles. Kitamura's kick can best be described as a continuous 123123123, but it is very interesting to find that the 1,500 m winner Terada in 1936 was using a leg action with a resting phase. We shall have more to say later about this 'resting phase' in the leg action.

Because of the generally small stature of the Japanese, with rounded shoulders and short legs with well developed calves, the stroke they evolved has probably with good reason, been called a 'masterpiece of adaptation.' It is a style well suited to the body build of most Japanese, who are not tall and broad-shouldered like Weissmuller and Devitt, with their tapering bodies.

Takaishi in the book *Swimming in Japan*, published in 1935, wrote an article on the crawl-stroke explaining the Japanese line of thought, and what he said *then* is still worthy of careful study today. I believe it is an excellent analysis:

'There are a few who have the opinion that the pressing movement of the arm at the beginning of the stroke is of no use or can even be detrimental for increasing speed, but the writer believes that this very movement decides whether one is a good swimmer or not. A good swimmer must learn to press the water skilfully. It is better to let the arm into the water before it is completely extended. If one extends the arm fully before letting it into the water, the time for pressing will be too long.

'Both shoulders draw ellipses while swimming. One of them should be lifted when the other is dropped. Accordingly, the upper part of the body should roll to both sides, but the position of the body line does not change. This movement is called rolling the body and it has a very close relation with the crawl stroke. If one swims without rolling the body on the longitudinal axis he must swim in a very un-natural position, such as pushing the head above the surface of the water or floating the upper part of the body by sinking the legs deeply in order to breathe easily.

'If one tries to stroke without rolling the body the power required is produced only by the muscles of the arms and shoulders, but when the power of the rolling of the body is added to that of the arms the force will be greatly increased. But one must understand that there is a limit even for rolling, as too much will destroy the form or will slow down the stroke. Rolling of the body is necessary and the power produced by it greatly strengthens the stroke when it is combined with the arm movements. This strength is increased according to the degree of rolling, consequently it is natural that the more one rolls the body, the larger the arm movement becomes. The larger the movement, the slower the tempo of the stroke.

'The best method of speed swimming for a fixed distance is to swim with the largest and strongest stroke and with as high a tempo as possible. However it is difficult for a swimmer of limited power and strength to enlarge his stroke without dropping his tempo. Thus, we must consider the limit of rolling. In considering this it is important to decide whether the rolling suits a swimmer or not for on this deci-sion rests whether he will succeed. This limit cannot be decided uniformly for every person. It is very difficult to find the limit of rolling which is most suitable for each individual. If one rolls the body too much he is compelled to let the arm stop while pressing on the water before it commences the catching movement.

'In short, the maximum of rolling is when the power gained by that rolling is all applied to the arm movement and each arm carries on its stroke without wasting time and energy.

'If the secret of speed swimming is to swim with the largest and strongest strokes and at the highest tempo, then the ideal would be for one with great strength to swim a certain distance with very strong strokes of the arms without rolling of the body because rolling drops the tempo.

'It is more understandable to call the pressing movement the sup-porting movement. One may think that this movement is done only by hand and wrist but in the crawl-stroke every part of the arm must press the water and even the shoulder helps this movement.

'It is the power of the finishing movement of the arms which actually increases the speed. Consequently the finishing movement should be done very quickly and strongly.

'While an arm is above the surface of the water it is of no use for increasing the speed. At this time the arm should be relaxed, and the only effort should be raising the elbow by using the muscles of the shoulder.

'The form of the arm recovery varies in each individual, but in general the best form is this – lift up the elbow after an arm finishes the stroke movement and take it out of the water as if pulling the hand with the elbow. Carry it forward drawing a circle with the shoulder as the centre and extend the arm forward and straighten the elbow when it is parallel with the body line. If one takes this method, the hand from the point of catching traces a parallel line with the central line of the body. Even though the hand is let into the water before the elbow is straightened one can bring it to the proper position by straightening the elbow in the water. Even the highest tempo cannot affect the position.

'Inhaling is done at the moment the roll on the breathing side is at its height. When the arm of the breathing side is near the end of its pull, gradually begin to turn up the face sideways and finish breathing when the arm makes its last snap, because at this time the rolling of the body is at full swing. Then the face must be carried back to its former position as the arm is carried forward. The mouth must be above the surface of the water for as short a time as possible. Then one must inhale through the mouth as much as possible in that short time. Then hold the air and exhale little by little until the mouth appears again above the water.'

Shozo Makino, only 5 feet 1 inch tall and weighing 8½ stone (119 lb.) one of Japan's outstanding swimmers and holder of the world record for 800 m and runner-up to Kitamura in the 1,500 m at Los Angeles, made these interesting and provocative comments:

'I pull out my hand before it has completed the stroke and stretch out immediately, not stroking to my waist thoroughly. This form is the best to keep a fast pace without much weariness in a long distance race. However, the form of long distance swimmer Honda, who won the Japanese and world records for the 1,000 m in 1934 is not that of a high tempo but that of long large strokes. I do not know which form is best, but each swimmer should choose that which suits him. The most important and common point is that the swimmer

F

has to push the water firmly away as soon as he puts his hands in, *without resting.*'

It is interesting that although the predominant feature of their stroke of the 1930s was usually interpreted as a *long glide* combined with a strong, continuous leg action and this was the stroke 'borrowed' by many *un*successful Australian swimmers at this time, the top Japanese coaches and swimmers were stressing the need to drive the arms quickly and firmly through the water using *very little* glide. When I read what the Japanese coaches said about crawl technique in the 1930s I appreciate that today my understanding of what is good technique is very much along these lines.

CHAPTER FIFTEEN

More Experiments in Style

THE Japanese men were nearly as successful at the Berlin Olympics in 1936 as they had been four years earlier. This time they took ten places, to five by the U.S.A.

The American Jack Medica won the 400 m from the Japanese Uto and Makino, whilst the two Japanese sprinters, Yusa and Arai, were touched off by the Hungarian Ferenc Csik in the 100 m. In women's events the American freestylers were toppled by *Dutch* girls, led by Rie Mastenbroek who won the 100 m and 400 m in Olympic record times of 1 minute 5.9 seconds and 5 minutes 26.4 seconds.

In Europe, during the 1930s, swimmers with a low flat position in the water who stretched the arms well forward in the recovery were meeting with success, and in America the tall, heavily-built Jack Medica also swam in a very horizontal position. As a schoolboy, I remember overhearing Medica saying in 1937 – when he visited Australia – that it was best to 'swim down-hill.' James Christy (U.S.A.) and Noel Ryan (Australia), third and fourth in the 1,500 m at Los Angeles, were other successful swimmers who swam low in the water with flat body positions. Both stretched the arms well out for their initial push down on the water.

On the other hand the slender, tapering Ferenc Csik of Hungary was a sprinter with a combination of pronounced back hollowing and very high alternate lifting of the shoulders. In the recovery, rather than swinging his arms around in the Weissmuller fashion, the Hungarian used more of a throw forward with moderately bent elbows. His hands entered the water in front of his head, to make a fairly straight-armed pull under the body on the centre line.

Csik's breathing was irregular, but it was *not* of the alternate side, bi-lateral type introduced by Jean Taris and also used by

163

Barany, the earlier Hungarian sprinter.

Holland's Willy den Ouden, who reached her best in 1932 when she swam second in the 100 m at Los Angeles, also adopted the Weissmuller technique of hollow-back and high upper body position, but her very successful team-mate, Rie Mastenbroek, was using a different method.

Rie Mastenbroek used a flat-body position with her face well down in the water. Having good flexibility she was able to lift each shoulder remarkably high during the arm recovery. Her recovery action of the arm was something new. It was made with high elbows and with the forearm kept *in front of* the elbows as the hand was, as it were, pushed forward. The arms were stretched well out, freely and quickly, before beginning the press down on the centre line. The other arm pushed well back. The legs with a powerful drive seemed, like Jean Taris', to have a considerably up-thrust component. For many years the Dutch coaches have taught the need of the up-thrust in the leg action.

The Danish girl Ranghild Hveger, second to Mastenbroek in the 400 m at Berlin, took practically all the women's world records at freestyle during the next three years. She reduced the 400 m mark to 5 minutes 0.1 second (made in a 25 m course) and the 800 m to 10 minutes 52.5 seconds. With a slight hollowing of the back, Hveger used the high lift of the shoulder girdle with each arm recovery, but unlike Mastenbroek there was little 'peaking' of the elbows instead the recovery was low, and close to the water. The recovery arm was bent and the hand kept in front of the elbow throughout the recovery, which was made with a quick motion. The hand entered the water just in front of the shoulder, stretching forwards and downwards like the Japanese. The leg action of both Hveger and Mastenbroek could best be described as independent up-thrust 'flutters,' made with straight legs and toes turned in.

We saw Ranghild Hveger conclude a remarkable career in 1952, when she swam fifth in the final of the 400 m at the Helsinki Olympics in 5 minutes 16.9 seconds.

After the Berlin Games came the second world war, and it was twelve years before the Olympic Games were revived in London in 1948. In the meantime, by 1942 practically all the freestyle world records from 200 m to 880 yards were held by the thickly-set 16 stone (224 lb) Hawaiian, Bill Smith.

The Modern American Crawl

Smith swam with a flat body position and a regular six-beat stroke which the famous Yale coach Bob Kiphuth described in 1942 in his widely read book *Swimming*. The stroking technique that Kiphuth recommended at this time was used by most American champions in the period 1940 to 1956.

Kiphuth felt that the arm action for the ideal stroke lay between what he termed the 'short' Japanese and the 'stretched out' American style. *It was a six-beat kick for all distances.* This is how Kiphuth described the style he felt subjectively represented the most efficient freestyle:

'The body should be in a perfectly flat position with head and chest fairly high, the water level above the eyes; shoulders level with the surface of the water and the horizontal axis through the shoulders should be at right angles to the long axis of the body. This means, ideally, that there should be *no* dipping of the shoulders or rolling of the body; neither should there be lunging nor hunching of one shoulder ahead of the other. The arms should move in the shoulder joint, but the shoulder itself should be in a fixed position, the body moving over the arms, literally "crawling."

'Care must be taken not to allow the catch and pull to be too wide because such a position cannot take advantage of the strong muscle pull that is possible with the arms near the middle line of the body. On the other hand a pull *across* the middle line of the body under the body is *incorrect* because in this position a great deal of water must be slipped in recovery since the arm has to be moved outwards and in such an action the backward push of the water at the end of the stroke is lost.'

Kiphuth described the arm recovery of this stroke as being made with a bent elbow, the hand covering a semi-circular path. The arms extended forward beginning the press down with *a raised wrist*.

The *leg* action was a regular and relatively deep six-beat.

For the sake of classification we may call this stroke described by Kiphuth the Modern American Crawl.

I must say here and now that in my opinion the 1942 version of the American crawl – with its deep six-beat kick and flat body position – which was used widely up to 1956 is now obsolete, nearly as *passé* as the side-stroke.

London 1948

Most nations, particularly European countries, found themselves unprepared for the London Olympic Games and with the recent memories of war, Japan was not permitted to compete in 1948.

The U.S.A. took eleven of the eighteen possible swimming places in men's events. Although a number of Olympic records were set, when we considered the times of all the finalists, the general standard had not risen since the Berlin Olympics. I remember making an analysis on the sea voyage back to Australia and nearly convincing myself that swimming records had just about reached a plateau and only slight improvements might be expected from here. How wrong this idea was to prove in the ten years that followed!

In the 100 m sprint at Wembley Swimming Stadium, the tall Walter Ris defeated his fellow-American Alan Ford, who was then the 100-yards world record holder. Bill Smith completed a grand swimming career by an all the way win in the 400 m from Jim McLane.

The three Americans Ris, Ford and Smith, used the modern American crawl described by Kiphuth, and Jim McLane, who won the 1,500 m for America, differed only in that he lifted his elbows slightly more in the recovery and had a somewhat shorter entry gliding longer before the arm drive. When I pulled out some dusty movie films I made of McLane in London and compared them with my films of today's champions, I was amazed at the extent of the glide and the regularity and depth of McLane's kicking.

John Marshall (Australia) and Gyorgy Mitro (Hungary) were placed behind McLane in the 1,500 m. They used individual and rather different techniques. John Marshall went on to greater things and his stroking technique was most interesting.

John Marshall swam with a well-arched back and a very effective, shallow flutter kick. He used a remarkably high lift of his flexible shoulders on each arm recovery, which was made with high elbows and an outwards flick of the forearm. This took the arm to an almost completely extended position in front of the shoulders. His whole stroke was characterised by his extreme flexibility.

In 1951 Marshall swam the 400 m in 4 minutes 26.9 seconds, and eventually claimed almost every world record from 200 m to the mile. Besides his extreme flexibility, Marshall had another important physical characteristic – very high tolerance for blood acidity. Professor T. K. Cureton reports in his book *The Physical Fitness of Champion Athletes* (Uni. of Illinois Press 1949) that when Marshall was tested in the laboratory at Illinois, he was found to rank higher than any sportsman previously measured in this capacity to tolerate the build-up in the blood of lactic acid, the fatigue product of exercise.

Within six months of joining Kiphuth at Yale, the 19-year-old Marshall – following three months of conditioning exercises and pulley-weight work – had built up from 152 lb. to 172 lb. I still have a letter Marshall sent me at that time. He said that instead of the one mile per day training he had averaged in Australia, he was swimming up to six miles on many days, and carrying out a great deal of this at close to full speed. He spoke of the personality and immense drive of Kiphuth.

Marshall was killed tragically in a motor car accident soon after the 1956 Olympic Games where he finished fifth in the 200 m butterfly-stroke final.

In 1949 and the early 1950s a 5 feet 9 inches, 11½ stone Japanese student of the Nihon University turned the spotlight on his country when he vied with John Marshall for being the world's fastest distance swimmer. Hironoshin Furuhashi reduced the 1,500 m record to 18 minutes 19 seconds.

Furuhashi swam with a technique which created great interest at the time and has a number of lessons to teach us today. His style was quite unlike the conquering Japanese freestylers of the 1930s, in fact it was unlike anything the world had seen before in championship swimming.

Furuhashi had a stroke of his own. He made very good use of the extremely powerful muscles of his upper body in a continually moving arm action. His shoulders and body rolled considerably as he drove the shoulder into each arm stroke. The arms speared into the water close to his head and pulled under the body without any apparent glide.

His feet barely broke the surface, and close examination

showed an unusual underwater action. When I saw him in the
North Sydney Olympic Pool his leg action could be classified as
a four-beat with one particularly large downward flip of his
right leg, made with a well-bent knee just as the left arm speared
into the water.

There were *two* major beats, one with each leg, just before
each arm started on the major part of its drive and two small
flutters. When he saw Furuhashi in an exhibition with John
Marshall at Yale in 1950 this is what Bob Kiphuth said:

'The secret of his (Furuhashi's) technique lies in the development of his arms. The Furuhashi style does *not* reflect
any new or revolutionary trend in Japanese swimming as a
whole.

'He is absolutely unique – in a class by himself. He couldn't
have copied the style from anyone else and no one else could
copy it even if they wanted to.'

However, I believe that Furuhashi's style was the straw in the
wind. His was the forerunner of later successful techniques.

Handy's Underwater Pictures

The American engineer Jamison Handy saw something new
and exciting in the Furuhashi style. Handy, a good swimmer
himself, played an important part in the evolution of swimming,
experimenting successfully with the 'legless' crawl during the
early 1900s. He never ceased to be a student of the sport. Handy
made a very significant contribution to swimming when in 1950
he maintained that the Furuhashi stroke was far from being a
crude and 'freak' mode of progression, and did in fact represent
an important new advance pointing the way to improving the
crawl as a speed stroke.

Handy had taken underwater stroboscopic pictures at .004 of
a second of outstanding American swimmers of the period, all
regular six-beat Modern American Crawl swimmers. A careful
study of these pictures established that such was the depth of the
kick and nature of the six-beat timing that for every cycle of the
arms there were two periods of foot *drag*. This occurred at the
time of maximum acceleration of the stroke, when the arms
were just beyond half way in the pull. There were thus two

moments when the legs 'put on the brakes' in each complete revolution of the arms. This braking effect is increased when the speed from the arms is added to the speed obtainable on the kicking board alone and may explain why the speed of the *whole* stroke is no simple relation between speed obtained from arms and legs separately.

Another important consideration is that a regular deep six-beat kick did not allow for any resting phase in the leg action which employs the large muscle groups of the thighs and legs. A leg action involving less than the six-beat thrash would theoretically give a greater period of rest for the legs, allowing blood to flow more freely through the working muscles in their relaxation phase.

Yet another result of the leg action being less than a regular six-beat – and I believe this is very important – is that the arms can go straight into their drive with less of a glide, less waiting in front for the legs to fit in the three beats with each single arm cycle. Although at first sight his very individual stroke appeared ugly and unusual, Furuhashi was experimenting in a practical way with something radically new in swimming technique – and it worked well enough to give him all world records from 400 m to 1,500 m. Being wise after the event, we can now see the reason. Furuhashi employed the important principle of 'four-cycle propulsion,' evening out acceleration within each arm cycle. Each major leg kick was made at a time *early* in the catch before maximum propulsion came from the driving arm. This meant that the propulsive movement came in an alternate manner from each arm and leg, and that during the most propulsive part of the arm drive the feet and legs were well within the streamline of the body.

There was something else very interesting about Furuhashi. He was born near Lake Hamana, an area that for years has supplied most of Japan's swimming champions, where children learn to swim almost as soon as they can walk. It is here that youngsters often swim five or six miles out to one of the islands to picnic, with their lunches tied on their heads.

This rather confirms a theory of mine that the key to the problem of producing super-swimmers of tomorrow may be in taking very young children and scientifically 'dosing' them with the exercise of swimming as they grow. Starting even at 9 or 10

years of age may in future prove to be far too late for the best
possible performances. It is a case of, 'as a twig is bent so will it
grow,' and the earlier the organism is trained to swim the better
may be the final result in terms of swimming speed.

Helsinki 1952

The Helsinki Games in 1952 saw all Olympic records broken
and a far higher general standard than in London. Furuhashi,
who 'had to work and could not train as hard as before,' and
John Marshall, who I believe trained *too hard* at the wrong time,
were both failures at Helsinki, barely qualifying for finals. The
American men and the Hungarian girls were the most successful.
The slim 19-year-old, 6 feet 2 inches French youth, Jean Boiteux,
won the 400 m, using his large and flexible feet to make a shallow
continuous flutter kick. He swam with high elbows and a fairly
short arm entry.

The Americans, Clarke Scholes and Ford Konno, who won
the 100 m and the 1,500 m respectively, were typical modern
American six-beat swimmers. Scholes had been photographed
underwater by Jamison Handy and was shown to have the deep,
'dragging' six-beat action.

I have examined underwater movies of Ford Konno, the 5 feet
$6\frac{1}{2}$ inches 10 stone Hawaiian who, by the Helsinki Games, had
broken most of Furuhashi's and Marshall's world records. The
flat shoulders and recovery, with stretched out arms and raised
wrists, the glide before the arm pull, and the deep six-beat kick
of the American crawl were all obvious. Konno set a new
Olympic record of 18 minutes 30.3 seconds for the 1,500 m.

However, as far as America and Europe were concerned the
failure of Furuhashi and the success of the Americans served
to confirm in many people's minds the 'fact' that the orthodox
Modern American Crawl with the six-beat kick was still the
'ideal' stroke. Kiphuth wrote after the Games:

'It is impressive to see most of the Helsinki competitors
using *accepted* styles of swimming. There was very little windmill action in freestyle recovery with the majority using a
bent arm and riding with an even, *flat* body position.'

We saw nothing new in the freestyle techniques of the winners at the Olympics in 1952. Swimmers and coaches went home to prepare for 1956, when the Olympic Games were to go to the Southern Hemisphere for the first time in history. It was in Melbourne that Australian freestylers scooped the pool and swimming standards made the greatest-ever leap forward in the space of one Olympiad.

CHAPTER SIXTEEN

The Australian Revival

AUSTRALIA's big move forward in swimming came to a climax with the 1956 Games in Melbourne. The promise of the early 1950s was fulfilled. Australians won every freestyle event and took the first *three* places in both men's and women's 100 m sprints.

Jon Henricks, Lorraine Crappe, David Theile, Murray Rose and Dawn Fraser swept all before them, and the world asked – Why? As one of the coaches to the 1956 Australian team, here is the explanation for the success of our swimmers as I see it.

Basically, I believe that the Australians *trained harder* and *swam with better techniques than their rivals*. They were the product of a swimming programme well advanced for its time – but soon to be successfully copied in principle by the Americans and later by many Europeans. Australian coaches and officials encouraged boys and girls to train hard and to race from the early age of eight and even younger.

Since 1900, Australia, with its favourable climate and high standard of living, has had more than its share of top world swimmers . . . except for one lean period during the 1930s, when most coaches were teaching bad imitations of Japanese techniques by concentrating on heavy leg action and glide in the arm action, and officials and swimmers seemed to spend their time lamenting the fact that Australia did not have the indoor swimming facilities enjoyed by the Americans.

Then in the early 1950s a few professional coaches, led by Harry Gallagher and Frank Guthrie, entirely on their own initiative and usually at odds with the Australian Swimming Union, developed a group of swimmers who startled the world.

Swimming outdoors for five months of the year in pools crowded with the public, by 1954 a few Australians were demonstrating that top swimmers *could* be developed by Australian coaches under local conditions.

Behind the scenes, always coming up with new ideas, was Professor Frank Cotton. Himself once N.S.W. 440-yard and 880-yard champion, he was a Doctor of Science and the Professor of Physiology at the University of Sydney.

For nearly fifteen years I had the privilege of working with 'Prof.' Cotton (who died in 1955) as his right hand man in swimming matters. During this period I was a competitive swimmer, an amateur coach and a lecturer in Physiology at the University. Australia – indeed all the swimming world – owes Professor Cotton a great deal. Many modern training procedures as used in Australia today (and much has now found its way overseas), were pioneered by our group of swimmers at the North Sydney Olympic Pool, including such people as John Davies, Nancy Lyons and Judy Joy Davies, all Olympic medal winners. As far back as 1947 they studiously kept their *log books* written up, an idea that has now spread everywhere. Today at North Sydney Olympic Pool you will still find one of the *first* large minute clocks to be used for the day-by-day training of swimmers. We installed this clock for experimental purposes in 1946. Nowadays, such clocks are used all over the world. We introduced the idea of repeat 'efforts,' took heart rates to appraise these training swims, put swimmers into hot baths to warm up for races, and used Interval Training. At the time we met with a fair amount of criticism for our methods as being unnecessary, 'scientific hocus-pocus,' but now most of these things are accepted as commonplace.

However, it was the professional coaches – Guthrie, Gallagher and Herford and later Don Talbot with his two Konrad stars – who showed us *just how hard* swimmers could be worked in training. It took me a number of years to be convinced that, with certain reservations, swimmers *must* be driven very hard in their training, almost unmercifully, if world records are to be made. Today this need for very hard training is even more evident, *but* with the reservations we have already discussed in our considerations of testing, tapering off, and stress and strain.

We saw a preview of what was to follow when Lorraine Crappe made a world record for 880 yards of 11 minutes 0.2 seconds in 1954 while training at Townsville. This was just the start. By 1960 Australians had broken more than *sixty* world records in all styles.

In addition to the enthusiasm of coaches and swimmers, and of course hard training, I believe that Australian successes at the crawl-stroke during the 1950s were due to the general use of a technique which might well be called the *modern* Australian Crawl-stroke.

Of course, not all the Australians swam exactly alike. In fact two in particular, Lorraine Crappe and John Devitt, had quite individual styles, but *in general* there were many characteristics common in this group of Australians who set the world wondering in the mid-1950s. In the next chapter we shall discuss the freestyle techniques of the modern Australian swimmers.

CHAPTER SEVENTEEN

Australian Crawl-stroke Today

THE two most important factors which have influenced today's 'Australian Crawl' are that swimmers have made their arms dominate the stroke minimising the part played by the legs, and that exercises and weight training have been carried out during the six months 'off-season' to increase flexibility and develop and strengthen the muscles of the arms and upper body.

If there was any *one* model for the Australians (particularly in the arm recovery), it was probably the great American swimmer Johnny Weissmuller, but there was one big difference in the Australians' approach – they trained very much harder than Weissmuller or his coach ever thought possible.

Characteristically, the legs of the Australians made a fairly narrow fluttering action, very much shallower than the deep thrashing kicks used by the Americans in 1952 at the Helsinki Games. Australians, like Dawn Fraser, Jon Henricks and Lorraine Crappe, all kept their leg actions narrower and much more within the streamline of the body. Their feet were kept well 'pointed,' helping to cut down resistance.

The leg kicks of the Australians were *not* regular six-beats. Nearly all Australians, even Crappe, Fraser and Henricks, who at first sight appeared fairly orthodox, could be seen to have a type of 'irregularly continuous' leg action on closer analysis. Each swimmer had his own particular irregularity in the leg kick, as for example a diagonal movement of one foot while the opposite arm recovered. Murray Rose, for instance, used a definite trailing action with his legs in races of more than 100 m. During distance swims underwater movies I have taken show that Rose at times has used a two-beat action, but generally he has a distinct four-beats in 400 m events and an 'irregular' five-beat action for 100 m and 200 m sprints. John Devitt (second in the 100 m at the Melbourne Olympics and winner of the gold medal

175

at Rome) had a very inefficient and relatively inactive leg kick, because his ankle joints were not at all supple. Devitt would take a long time, about 70 seconds, to kick a board 55 yards, whereas Lorraine Crappe, who had the strongest leg action of any Australian of this period, could beat all the men at kicking. I once timed her at 37 seconds for 55 yards.

The 'secret' of the successful Australian crawl-stroke in recent years lies in the fact that whether or not the individual's leg kick was a strong one, the arm action was always considered by far the most important factor in the stroke. Usually more arms only (pulling) practice with a band around the ankles was carried out than kicking-board practice. Coaches believed that the legs must 'dance' attendance on the arms *not* vice-versa. This is why arms-only work is given an important place in our training. When we went to Holland to coach in 1962 we had the greatest difficulty in persuading coaches and swimmers that, compared to the arms, the leg kick was relatively unimportant, and that a swimmer who *over*-kicked was spoiling himself in this way.

If you look carefully at many of the world's fastest crawl swimmers today, particularly in distances over 100 m, you will be able to distinguish what I call a '*broken-tempo*' in the leg action.

With all my pupils (both sprinters and distance swimmers) I have gone so far as to insist on *some* trailing action of the legs, a momentary one or two pauses with the legs during each cycle of the arms. Few, if any of my pupils, kick with what would be described as a regular six-beat, and no two of them kick in quite the same way.

To the best of my knowledge it was Dr Jim Counsilman, coach at Indiana, who first made a scientific analysis of the *cross-over* kick in the same way as Professor Cureton had made a masterly analysis of the six-beat flutter kick in 1930. Counsilman's paper followed observation and experiments with George Breen, the Olympic 1,500 m record-holder until 1960.

In discussing the so-called *ugly* legs-crossing style of his pupil Breen, Jim Counsilman once told me how, in Breen's early days, he used to over-hear swimming 'authorities' at swim-meets saying that 'the boy might make a good swimmer *if* he got a good coach and learned better style' (meaning that he should kick a six-beat).

However, Counsilman showed, not only with Breen but also with other top crawl swimmers, such as Alan Sommers, that those with low flexibility of the shoulder joint causing a wide arm recovery will tend to swing their buttocks from side to side and that to prevent this resistance it is very much better for these inflexible swimmers to allow the legs to make a compensatory crossing-over action which counter-acts the swing of the hips.

In the early 1950s American coaches in general had seemed to agree with Bob Kiphuth's opinion expressed in his book *Swimming* – that in the crawl-stroke the 'body should lie perfectly flat . . . and there should be no dipping of the shoulders or rolling of the body.' Yet most top Australian swimmers *were* permitted to dip their shoulders and they *did* roll their bodies. In fact the bodies of most of the Australian swimmers in recent years have rolled considerably *around their longitudinal axis.* This rolling movement includes shoulders, hips and legs, in contrast to the Japanese of the 1930s who did not roll the hips. The fact that the shoulder digs down into the water generally means that the muscles of the trunk (as well as the arm muscles) can be brought into action in the pull through. This shoulder movement was where the Australians differed from Weissmuller, who swam in a flatter position and somewhat higher in the water.

Many top Australians in recent years have swum with a fairly horizontal position and have not made a conscious effort to get head and chest up high. Murray Rose has always swum well *down* in the water. I believe that the key to maintaining this horizontal position lies in *turning* rather than lifting the head for a breath, and keeping the water-line across the top of the head *not* 'just above the eyes,' as many coaches and swimming books still teach today. The breathing technique used by Rose, Crappe, Fraser and other great Australians is uncomplicated. The head is kept down, turning to breathe and coming back to the front again in time with the roll of the shoulders. Inhalation is made through the mouth and exhalation through the mouth and nose.

At Rome in 1960 I saw two very fine American sprint swimmers whose heads were even lower in the water and bodies more horizontal than the Australians. They were Lance Larson, who was awarded second place to John Devitt in the 100 m, and Jeff Farrell, who made athletic history by competing three weeks after having an appendix operation.

G

I believe that one of the great fallacies in teaching crawl-stroke has been the story that, by getting up on top of the water 'like a speed boat' the swimmer will cut down resistance and be faster. No swimmer will ever be able to exert the power necessary to plane over the water like a boat. All he will do by striving to 'get up high' in the water is to incline his body at an angle and *increase* resistance, thus wasting energy. For all styles of swimming this same principle holds. With my pupils, I often give the example of the submarine which, using the same power, is faster when completely under the water than when it is half submerged. When the water-line runs across the shoulders resistance and wave-making will be greatest, just like the submarine half submerged.

My advice to swimmers, for all styles of swimming, is to lie down in the water and stay as horizontal as possible in order to cut down resistance. We have good examples of this in such great swimmers as Murray Rose at crawl-stroke, Chet Jastremski at breast-stroke, and Tom Stock at back-stroke. All of these champions have used the greater part of the power they generate to propel them forward and along, *not* to get up on top of the water.

Now let's look at the arm action for crawl swimming.

The Australians during their 'revival' in the 1950s almost all used the bent arm, boomerang-like swing for the recovery similar to the unique American, John Weissmuller. The straight arms of the Hungarians and the typical American stretch-out recovery with cupped hands and high wrists were both rejected. Instead, the Australians kept the hand distinctly lower than the elbow on entry and from then on there was very little glide as the hand took a hold on the water and pressed down and then back. An exception was Lorraine Crappe, the girl with the particularly powerful and flexible leg action, which drove her forward over a distinct glide in the arm action before she began to pull.

In general, the Australian under-water action was for the arm to take an S-shaped, weaving path about the centre line. We have long interpreted a pull straight through the water without the S as indicating the inefficient technique of 'cutting holes in the water.' Dawn Fraser and a number of other top swimmers have allowed the hands to wander well across the centre line during the pull. Most Australians bent their elbows considerably

during the arm-pull, taking pains to make a distinct push back
at the end, not just to the hips but to the thighs.

Whereas the Americans of the early 1950s generally used a
stroke where the arms glided in front for an appreciable period,
most Australians drove their arms quickly down and pulled with
very little waiting in front. As Counsilman has said – 'While
you are gliding you are resting and your rival may be pulling.'
The Australians did not do too much resting with their arms,
they pulled.

Now we come to a most important point in the crawl-stroke –
the action of the legs. In the orthodox crawl, with a regular six-
beat kick to each complete arm cycle, it is necessary to wait
momentarily with each arm extended in front in order to fit in
the leg beats before the arms can push firmly down and back.
With an irregular *broken-tempo* and a pause in the leg action,
each arm can start pressing down firmly immediately it enters
the water. This, to my mind, is the most important reason why
this type of irregular leg-action is effective.

We tell our pupils to push down from the surface, keeping the
elbow a little higher than the hand. I think it was the American
coach, Matt Mann who said, 'Push down, don't pull back.' This,
I believe, is excellent advice. After the initial push down with a
relatively straight arm, the pulling arm will quite naturally begin
to bend at the elbow, enabling more muscles to be brought into
action. Counsilman calls this the *rotating action* of the forearm.

The principle of a high elbow throughout the arm drive is
important because it allows more resolved force to be used for
forward propulsion and is much more efficient than a weak
elbow-*down* movement made with an extended arm.

It might be said that none of these points of style favoured by
the top Australians in recent years was new or original, and
after reading the foregoing chapters you will agree that most
things have been tried before. However, I believe the particular
combination of these points was something new. Many points of
technique were not first worked out carefully on paper by
coaches and *then* applied: they gradually evolved while the
emphasis was being placed on swimmers carrying out very
strenuous interval training.

My wife and I made a Commercial 16 mm. Instructional film
on the swimming techniques of champions, including Austra-

lians, and we were able to compare the slow-motion shots of Murray Rose taken in 1957 with the Murray Rose technique of 1962 (soon after he had returned from America where he had just made his new 400 m world record of 4 minutes 13.4 seconds). It was clear that in 1962 Murray was stretching his arms out much further than he had before, thus he was able to make a longer pull. In addition, he began his elbow-bend earlier. I believe that these two changes were improvements in Rose's technique. Australian swimmers in recent years, like Rose in 1957, have tended to dive their arms too steeply into the pulling position. They certainly eliminate glide but often shorten their strokes unnecessarily by trying too hard to make a quick pull.

Perhaps the most efficient action lies somewhere between the complete stretch-out and the steep dive-down arm action that is seen in a number of Australian swimmers.

John Devitt, with a best time of 54.6 seconds, used an amazingly high stroking rate for his 100 m sprints. In order to get this high tempo he carried his arms over the water lower and straighter than most Australians, and he held his shoulders much flatter in the water. I believe that for top *sprinting* both these things are necessary to some degree. There should be less roll by the sprint swimmer, not because of lower resistance (which is doubtful anyway) but because he can gain a higher stroking tempo with a more stable body.

Sometimes you will hear it said that the way the arms recover over the water does not matter because 'it is what you do under the water which is important.' I believe that the form of the arm recovery *is* important, because it can effect the whole pattern of the stroke, and the balance of the body.

In nearly all top *sprinters* today, the arms are almost *flung* over in what is called a free ballistic movement. However, in middle distance swimming, where the tempo is slower and the recovery a little more controlled, I believe the arms should come over with the elbows high enough to enable the weight of the arms to be transmitted as it were straight down through the upper arm to the shoulder. Most of the best modern-day middle distance swimmers (and Rose is an outstanding example), show this type of arm recovery. This action is not possible unless the body is rolled to some extent around its longitudinal axis.

Returning to the legs, it has been wrongly said that 'Carlile does not believe in kicking the legs.' Actually I am certain that an *efficient* leg action can help a swimmer greatly. The important thing is how the legs are used. Even when Murray Rose is making only two-beats to an arm cycle, he still gets a great deal of propulsion from those two whip-like kicks. His feet move vigorously, diagonally and downward. One or two shallow, powerful kicks made with flexible ankles, followed by a trailing action, are very much more help in propulsion than the regular heavy beats of the old six-beat crawl-stroke.

We have made a great deal of progress in technique by studying carefully just what champion swimmers have used successfully. When we look back we find that many great swimmers of the past *have* swum with techniques not unlike today's champions. As I have said in the opening paragraph of this chapter, the big difference between the performance of many old-time champions and those of today is due to the harder training done today and to the tremendous amount of out-of-the-water strengthening work carried out during the off-season.

It need hardly be said that there is *no* one 'correct' crawl-stroke technique. Even while attempting to follow the same principles, each individual will have his own 'style' of swimming. Body build, and the normal *posture* of the individual, influence technique greatly.

To my mind the most important principle in swimming the modern crawl-stroke is that the legs should play a secondary part in the stroke and should be used with some variety of 'broken-tempo.' The legs must not be permitted, by kicking a regular six- or eight-beat, to impose a gliding action on the arms.

Coaches will ask – 'What about youngsters just out of the beginner stage – what shall we teach *them* to do with their legs?'

This problem has concerned the teachers in our Swimming School at Ryde, and this is my advice. In the early stages, a great deal of training should be done on a kick-board, emphasising looseness of joints, shallow kick and pointed toes. Sometimes, to give some 'form' to the kick, it may even be necessary to teach beginners to count 1 2 3 – 4 5 6, but I prefer them to be taught a continuous fluttering action with no special accent. Then, as soon as the leg action becomes reasonably strong, we start with arms-only *pulling*. For weaker swimmers, the legs are held up with a cork or float tied to the ankles.

It is my experience that when pulling work is done, the arms are forced to take an early hold on the water to prevent the swimmer from sinking, and then the *broken-tempo* leg action and more or less glideless arm action is quickly learned. The swimmer who over-kicks and glides too much can often be re-educated into a broken-tempo by plenty of arms-only work.

Coaching for style is an art more than a science. By this I mean that we do not have hard and fast scientific principles to guide us all along the line. For instance, we have a great deal to discover on the hydrodynamics of swimming and the muscular actions involved. I have pointed out here, by describing the modern 'Australian style' and the reasons for it, the general nature of a technique which has proved successful. Of course, I have no doubt that we shall have to change some of our ideas in the future because swimming is a dynamic study and must keep on progressing.

CHAPTER EIGHTEEN

Modern Breast-stroke

Olympic Games – 200 *m*

Year	Name	Country	Time
1908	F. Holman	Great Britain	3 min. 9.2 sec.
1912	W. Bathe	Germany	3 min. 1.8 sec.
1920	B. Malmroth	Sweden	3 min. 4.4 sec.
1924	R. D. Skelton	U.S.A.	2 min. 56.6 sec.
1928	Y. Tsuruta	Japan	2 min. 48.8 sec.
1932	Y. Tsuruta	Japan	2 min. 45.4 sec.
1936	T. Hamuro	Japan	2 min. 42.5 sec.
1948	J. Verdeur (Butterfly, with breast-stroke kick)	U.S.A.	2 min. 39.3 sec.
1952	J. Davies (Butterfly, with breast-stroke kick)	Australia	2 min. 34.4 sec.
1956	M. Furukawa ('Underwater' breast-stroke)	Japan	2 min. 34.7 sec.
1960	W. Milliken (Orthodox breast-stroke)	U.S.A.	2 min. 37.4 sec.

BREAST-STROKE, the classical swimming stroke, has undergone many changes since the nineteenth century when it was the only stroke used in London for racing. Captain Matthew Webb breast-stroked his way across the English Channel in 1875.

The 'butterfly' arm recovery has come and gone (the rules saw to this just in time to prevent breast-stroke disappearing as a competitive stroke). We have also seen the 'high-sail' (shoulders high) technique rise and fall in popularity. Then we have seen breast-stroke races with competitors under the water most of the time, until the rules of swimming were changed in 1956 to allow only one arm movement and one leg kick under water after the start and turns.

Under Jim Counsilman a group of strong breast-strokers has been developed at the University of Indiana in recent years. The most outstanding of these, Chet Jastremski, previously a medley swimmer, only became proficient at the stroke after he was eighteen years of age. Jastremski's non-glide arm action and his method of breathing after the beginning of the arm stroke came more or less as a revival of a successful technique used by the Japanese years ago. In fact, the timing of the breathing has been claimed to be similar to that of Captain Matthew Webb.

Counsilman studied the stroke carefully and worked very successfully on the premise that the arms should contribute substantially to propulsion and that *the shoulders should be kept under the water* as much as possible during the arm pull. Further, he narrowed down the leg action until the feet make a tight circle, almost kicking straight backward with the knees held close together.

Working on this technique and carrying out a great deal of arms-only pulling, the short but muscular Jastremski was the first swimmer to break 2 minutes 30 seconds for the 200 m in the 50 m course. In the Jastremski stroke the arms make a fairly narrow circle, with the shoulders remaining low. The head is kept down until just before the final inward rotating action of the forearms at the end of the arm pull. Then the head is raised quickly for a breath – there is a definite head lift – and lowered again before the arms stretch forward. The leg-kick is made during the stretching forward motion. Notice that we call it a *stretch forward* rather than use the term 'glide.' At racing speed there is very little time for a pause in the stretched forward position. This type of breast-stroke allows a very high tempo with emphasis on the power in the arm pull, keeping the arm stroke well forward, the elbows barely coming back behind the line of the shoulders.

In Australia until recently most breast-strokers have given very little consideration to the question of the timing of their breathing. By good fortune the best swimmers have delayed the lifting of the head to breathe until after the start of the arm pull, but most of the poorer swimmers have tended to breathe too early, as they glided forward, well before the start of the arm pull. We have observed that this early breathing caused them to lift the shoulders which *increased* the wave-making and *decreased* efficiency.

In 1962 at Leipzig, I studied closely the top Russian male breast-strokers who took the first two places in the European championships. The Russians appeared to me to use the same general pattern as Jastremski, except that they made more use of the propulsion from their flexible legs and finished the arm pull with their elbows close to the body. The Russians breathed even later in the arm stroke than Jastremski.

The Japanese have long been a leading nation in breast-stroke. Ohsaki who was second at the Rome Olympics in 1960, like other recent Japanese swimmers, used a similar technique to that described above, but by 1961 and 1962 the leading Japanese breast-strokers were pausing with the hands under the chest – 'getting caught behind' as we call it. They have since altered their techniques to the Jastremski pattern, where any slight pause is in the stretched forward position, rather than at the end of the arm pull.

I believe that breaststroke times will come tumbling down now that a clear idea of the late-breathing technique becomes more widely used. When my wife and I returned from Europe and America in 1962, we insisted on practically all our breast-stroke pupils, including Marguerithe Ruygrok, using this technique. Fifteen-year-old Marguerithe, after making a big stroke change, quickly reduced her 110 yards time to 1 minute 21.4 seconds (the Australian junior record). All our young swimmers became much faster with the new later breathing technique.

In the past, as I have pointed out, many breast-strokers breathed as the arms came forward. This meant a rising body, *high* shoulders and greater resistance than when the shoulders were kept down during the arm pull. My pupil Terry Gathercole, who once held the 200 m and 220 yards world records at 2 minutes 36.5 seconds, although he breathed fairly early in the arm pull, swam with his head tilted high enough to enable the shoulders to remain low in the water throughout the stroke. With Terry I was not yet fully convinced that very strong arm work was of great importance in breast-stroke. After all he *was* the best in the world and one hesitates to alter what seems very successful. However, I now believe that Terry did not do enough arms-only training and because his leg action gave so much propulsion, I allowed him, wrongly, as I now believe, to stroke too short with his arms.

It took Chet Jastremski and the Russians to finally open our eyes to the benefits of this late breathing, low shoulders and arms dominant technique of breast-stroke swimming.

CHAPTER NINETEEN

Butterfly-Stroke

Olympic Results – 200 m

1956	W. Yorzyk	U.S.A.	2 min. 19.3 sec.
1960	M. Troy	U.S.A.	2 min. 12.8 sec.

WHEN in the mid-1930s the butterfly over-the-water arm recovery was introduced into orthodox breast-stroke races without breaking the rules, this revolutionary technique proved fast but extremely tiring. Hence it could only be used for short distances and people thought that it would be impossible to swim it for even the full 200 m. How reminiscent of the first use of the double over-arm and later the crawl-stroke! As with the crawl the new technique eventually proved successful when swimmers practised hard. Now, we have an eight-year-old pupil who swims a fast 220 yards *butterfly* all the way, with no difficulty, and I am sure that coaches all over the world will tell me of six-year-old butterflyers swimming 400 m!

The butterfly arm action used with the orthodox breast-stroke kick came to the height of its development in 1952 when the Australian John Davies won the 200 m breast-stroke at the Helsinki Olympics in 2 minutes 34.4 seconds. Following this the door was opened for tremendous progress when the butterfly-stroke was separated from breast-stroke and became the fourth competitive stroke of swimming. Now with the dolphin (vertical) leg action the best butterfly swimmers rival the speed of all but champion crawl swimmers.

After 1952 the dolphin leg action was generally used with the high-flung arm recovery popularised by the very supple Bill Yorzyk, or with the undulating mostly-under-the-water technique of the Hungarian, Tumpec. Then, before the 1960 Olympics at Rome, Mike Troy of Indiana, and his coach Jim Counsilman, played a very important part in the development of the butterfly-stroke. Much of the undulation and heavy leg kick were eliminated by Troy. Don Talbot, coach of Australians Neville Hayes and Kevin Berry, told me that during a visit to the U.S.A. he learned much about butterfly technique from Troy and Counsilman, and applied this knowledge to Hayes and Berry, both of whom later broke world records.

Troy in 1960 used a double-dolphin leg action, *two* downward leg kicks to each cycle of the arms. The correct timing of the leg kicks was reckoned to be very important, one kick was made as the arms entered the water and the second just before the arms came out of the water at the end of the pull. A common fault of butterflyers in making the two leg kicks is to pause with the arms gliding out in front, while both leg kicks are made. As in the other styles there is little time for gliding in the modern butterfly-stroke.

Mike Troy, still the best model for modern butterflyers, made his arm entry in a V-shaped position, wide of the centre line. He then pulled with bent arms and elbows kept higher than the hands.

As they drove under the body, the hands practically came together in their curved path before making their final push back to the thighs with a rotating action of the forearms.

Troy usually breathed every second arm stroke, although Hayes and Berry have favoured breathing on every stroke. Nearly all top butterflyers in recent years, including Troy, appear to me to breathe *late* in the arm pull. The effect of late breathing and of making one non-breathing arm stroke is to keep the shoulders down in the water and help keep the body horizontal. Of course, what the swimmer gains by this he loses to some extent by having to restrict the amount of air he can take during his race, but one-time world record-holder, Mary Stewart of Canada, swam her butterfly with *three* or *four* strokes to the one breath when I saw her sprinting the 100 metres. Ada Kok of Holland (the European champion and record-holder in 1962) was another irregular breather. In 1963 she swam 100 m in 66.1 s.

The most significant point about Troy's style, which I have seldom seen bettered in male swimmers, was his very horizontal body position, making for a minimum of resistance. There was little of the Tumpec undulating action of 'diving down' before making the arm pull. Troy did not use a deep leg kick. Under-

555555

water movies show clearly the shallowness and streamlining of his leg action. Troy's hips were held high.

The steadiness of the hips to my mind is one of the outstanding characteristics of a good butterfly technique. If the body is allowed to bend unduly either at the hips or along the back during the arm pull, then I believe it must mean that energy will be used in unnecessary bodily movement in the vertical plane rather than in forward propulsion. Moreover, movement in hips and back usually result in a reduction in the *tempo* of stroking.

The most popular leg action used by present-day butterfly swimmers is a regular two-beat. However I am by no means convinced that this will prove best in the long run.

The original *two-beat* Australian crawl kick was eventually improved upon. So, in the future, it may well be that, as in the crawl leg action, no two top swimmers will be similar in their butterfly kicks and we shall see a wide variety of leg actions used by champions. The two-beat timing may in fact disappear in outstanding butterflyers.

As with the crawl-stroke leg action, I believe we must make the kick in butterfly *secondary* to the arms. Yet this does not mean that the leg-kick is *un*important. As with the modern crawl kick, I believe that a shallow, whip-like action, in some variety of a broken-tempo, may be developed by the great butterfly swimmers of the future.

CHAPTER TWENTY

The New Back-stroke

Olympic Winners – 100 *m Back-stroke*

1908	A Bieberstein	Germany	1 min. 24.6 sec.
1912	W. Hebner	U.S.A.	1 min. 21.2 sec.
1920	W. Kealoha	U.S.A.	1 min. 15.2 sec.
1924	W. Kealoha	U.S.A.	1 min. 13.2 sec.
1928	G. Kojac	U.S.A.	1 min. 8.2 sec.
1932	M. Kiyokawa	Japan	1 min. 8.6 sec.
1936	A. Kiefer	U.S.A.	1 min. 5.9 sec.
1948	A. Stack	U.S.A.	1 min. 6.4 sec.
1952	Y. Oyakawa	U.S.A.	1 min. 5.7 sec.
1956	D. Theile	Australia	1 min. 2.2 sec.
1960	D. Theile	Australia	1 min. 1.9 sec.

ADOLPH KIEFER of the U.S.A. had a great influence on back-stroke technique after 1936, the year he won at the Berlin Olympic Games.

It is only in recent years that the majority of coaches have realised that the 'Kiefer' technique with low arm recovery, wide entry and *straight* arm pull is by no means the best technique for back-stroke swimming. The Americans, Stack and then Oya-kawa, swam with Kiefer's straight-arm pull when they won in London and Helsinki, but by 1956 Australia's David Theile, winner at Melbourne and then again at Rome, together with his countryman John Monckton, and Fred McKinny of America, left no doubt that there was a better technique for back-stroke swimming. These three great back-strokers swam in a markedly different way from Kiefer and the many swimmers he had influenced.

Instead of the low recovery, 'two o'clock' arm entry of Kiefer, the arms now recovered straight up and back, entering nearly on the centre line. Instead of pulling just under the surface and straight like an oar in the Kiefer manner, their arms first drove downwards, then when the hand was about a foot under water the arm began to bend and the water was pushed back with bent elbows. Towards the end of the arm stroke, there was a final rotation of the forearm and the hand usually finished its push with a downward movement somewhat below the level of the thigh. The bent elbow in the arm drive was the great change from the Kiefer back-stroke technique. The final downward action of the hand seemed to have the effect both of slightly lifting the shoulder on that side for the arm recovery and of throwing the other shoulder down on top of its arm drive.

The head was held back and the hips high, so that the body was quite horizontal. An important thing about the *head* action is that in the top back-strokers, even with some shoulder movement, it does not move around. The head is held firmly in position.

The new leg action was not heavy. I know that David Theile, two times Olympic winner, made some experiments in which he scarcely kicked and concluded that was best *not* to kick hard but to concentrate on arm work.

In recent years the American Tom Stock has been one of the greatest back-strokers. He is the big exception to the hydro-dynamic principle that sprint swimmers (100 m or 200 m) should be tall. Stock was 5 feet 6 inches high and weighed a little less than 140 pounds when we watched him train at Indiana University. It is amazing that this small fellow should have broken 61 seconds for 100 metres and been under 2 minutes 11 seconds for 200 m. His physique surely is against him and the explanation for his performances, to my mind, lies largely in his intensive pro-gramme of interval training and his excellent technique.

In Stock's back-stroke the body lies quite flat in the water with the head well back. The arms are thrown straight up and over, so that they appear to hit the water and push down and through without a pause. The arm drive is made with a bent arm and a distinct push back at the end of the stroke.

Stock's leg action when studied from underwater slow-motion movies interests me greatly because he certainly did *not* use the orthodox six-beat. Rather, he had a *broken-tempo* with a distinct pause allowing for a brief trailing leg action in each arm cycle. It is, in fact, just the type of action we have advocated for the crawl-stroke.

The broken-tempo, with the pause, enables the arms to make their entry into the water with a free swinging action. There is no glide, no waiting for the leg beats to fit in.

In Australia in recent years, it has been taught by some coaches that the head and shoulders should be held well up. In many swimmers this makes the body sink in the middle assuming a 'bath tub' position – then the body loses its horizontal position, violating the principle of good streamlining.

The Japanese back-stroker S. Tanaka, the first girl under 2 minutes 29 seconds for 220 yards and 200 m, swims with chin well forward but she still manages to keep her hips high and her body horizontal. With a relatively slow arm tempo she impresses me as having a wonderful 'feel' of the water.

In spite of what I have said about the bent arm pull, there are some outstanding girl swimmers who appear to pull with nearly straight arms, probably because their arms are relatively short.

Young children, when they first swim back-stroke, often pull with bent arms. Nature dictates the best way of using the muscles and now we see that science has added its blessing – some Russian research workers in physical education have written* a scientific paper showing that with this 'natural' bent-arm pull, more muscles can be thrown into action than when the arm is used straight. We so often find that first the swimmer discovers an efficient technique, then later we coaches can rationalise and, being wise after the event, explain *why* the technique is successful. So it has been with the modern back-stroke.

---

* An analysis of the arm movement in 'Swimming Back-stroke' by Dulinets, Duilovsky and Stepantsov. Translation in British Coaches Bulletin No. 18 ed. A. D. Kinnear.

CHAPTER TWENTY-ONE

The Secrets of the Tumble Turn and Start

IT is astonishing how many top-rate swimmers continually make bad turns and starts, depriving themselves of much of the benefit of their long and conscientious swimming training.

The fastest turn for sprints is the forward somersault or tumble turn, in fact it is not unusual today for 200 m and 400 m swimmers to make many of their turns in this way rather than the older middle-distance 'fall-back' method. At the European Championships in Leipzig (1962) we saw the young Spaniard, Miguel Torres, tumble efficiently for the complete 1,500 m, to take second place in that event.

Many European sprinters have for years used what they call the 'Kiefer' turn. Here the swimmer turns on to his back and then makes a somersault before pushing off. This turn is not as fast as the well-executed forward somersault because of the roll on to the back which breaks the continuity of the *forward* movement.

In recent years many of the top sprinters in the world have come from America and Australia and it has been obvious that the majority turn very well. Fundamentally the turning method for Australians and Americans is similar, except that many Australians somersault straight over while the Americans twist, to some extent, on to their sides as they *begin* the somersault. The Americans' legs may be said to 'flip' over more to one side, hence the American variety of the forward tumble is often called the Flip Turn.

Good tumble turning does not come easily. Without a clear idea of what he is trying to do a swimmer will never master the turn and will always be hesitant about using it, especially when under the pressure of a big race.

Here are the 'secrets' of tumble turning as my pupils and I have discovered them after a considerable amount of experiment, discussion and practical experience.

The turn can never be perfected in one or two lessons. We tell youngsters not to expect to tumble turn really well without at least six months' hard practice in training and in races.

After the swimmer has learned to make a forward somersault in the middle of the pool away from the wall, and is accustomed to feeling 'upside down,' we are ready to start practising the turn which is illustrated opposite page 152.

1. Aim to turn well *on the one arm*. We have found that with experience and practice a swimmer almost subconsciously seems to adjust his strokes to arrive at the wall on the same arm every time. At worst he has to make a short paddle-stroke with the opposite arm, or must glide and kick himself a foot or two in to the wall. Then he can always repeat the *same* turning pattern.

2. While kicking strongly towards the wall the arm should be *stretched* well out in front just under the surface of the water, at the same time the arm may be rotated inwards towards the centre-line of the body, so that the thumb is down and the palm of the hand faces outwards.

3. At the moment of *touching the wall* (you *must* touch or be disqualified), drop the shoulder *opposite* to the leading hand and push the head under the outstretched arm. Dropping the *opposite* shoulder is quite important.

4. The legs may then somersault almost *straight over* in the Australian manner, or flip over on the side of the body opposite the leading arm – as in the case of the Americans. Both methods can make for a fast turn.

5. During the somersault the body must bend at the hips and the legs should be nearly straight – there should be a minimum of tucking action. The legs should flick over well out of the water and almost *thud* into position on the wall.

6. The feet will usually land on the wall with the body on its side in both the Australian and American turns, but the Americans twist on to the side earlier than many Australians.

7. The push-off from the wall must be made from the position in which the feet hit the wall (preferably with the body on the

side rather than on the pack). There must be no time lost in twisting whilst in contact with the wall. For a fast turn the push-off must be immediate.

8. After the strong push-off there should be a short glide towards the surface. Then the legs should start kicking powerfully before the first stroke is made. The timing of exactly when to make the first stroke – indeed all the fine points of making a good tumble turn – will only come with practice. After about 3,000 attempts you should be close to mastering the skill of fast reliable tumble turning!

Starting

You will find starting dives discussed in detail in practically every swimming book. You will be told to take up a position with the feet comfortably apart (six to nine inches) to bend the knees slightly and lean forwards from the hips. All this is good advice, but it becomes confusing when some will tell you to have your arms *forward*, others say stretch them *back*, as you wait for the starter's gun. Personally I have favoured having the arms hanging almost straight down or in a slightly forward position, as though you are setting yourself to make a standing long jump.

Whatever the position of the arms the important thing is that on the starting signal they must immediately *swing forwards*, around and backwards. If there is any 'secret' of good starting then I believe that it is this immediate swing back. It is a law of physics that to every action there is an equal and opposite re-action. The arms swinging forceably *backwards* help quickly drive the body forwards into the dive. See opposite page 153.

A Final Word

This brings me to the end of my book on some of the important aspects of the competitive side of swimming.

Some of my readers may be tempted to use the instructions and ideas given here and believe they can dispense with a coach. If you do you can never expect to reach your best.

The ideal combination for success is to have a good, full-time coach and if possible to train with a squad of keen swimmers. The 'lone-wolf' is rarely successful nowadays. There is nothing quite like the stimulus of training with swimmers who are better than you are. Being one of a good team makes swimming much more interesting than doing it on your own.

Set your sights high. Nobody yet knows the limit of swimming performance. Young boys and girls today make the efforts of yesterday's champions seem paltry. So it will be in the future.

With new ideas, the application of more and more science, better coaching methods and the discovery of more young swimmers with outstanding ability, swimming records will continue to improve.

Even with all our present knowledge, no individual will accomplish much in swimming without years of persistent hard work and training, *and* without his share of disappointments. There are no short cuts to the top. You must develop good techniques, a strong, streamlined and flexible body, and great endurance. Nobody is *born* with these things. They must be worked for.

So go to it!

FORBES CARLILE,
Ryde Swimming Centre,
Sydney, Australia
August 1963